Book

" Drive "

Daniel H. Pink

Brockport &
Schoolcraft, LLC

Published by Brockport & Schoolcraft, LLC.
First Printing, 2012

ISBN-13: 978-0-9853680-1-2

Praise for Doctor's Eyes Only

"Doctor's Eyes Only should be required reading not only for young doctors, but for all young professionals and people with significant earning potential. Although I became associated with excellent financial advisors later in life, I wish I had read this book much earlier in my career. It is easy to understand and very practical."

—Dr. Benjamin S. Carson, Sr., Johns Hopkins Professor of Neurosurgery, Oncology, Plastic Surgery, and Pediatrics; Director of the Division of Pediatric Neurosurgery; Co-Director of the The Johns Hopkins Craniofacial Center; Award Winner of the Presidential Medal of Freedom; and Best-Selling Author

"Doctor's Eyes Only is the financial book I wish I would have read earlier in my professional career. It gave me a wonderful insight into managing finances that I never learned in surgical training. It is also tailored to my unique needs as a physician."

—Dr. Michael Lim, Johns Hopkins Assistant Professor of Neurosurgery and Oncology; Director of the Metastatic Brain Tumor Center; Director of Brain Tumor Immunotherapy

"Doctor's Eyes Only is a must-read for all medical residents and physicians early in their careers. This really is the missing business and financial course and I provide a copy to all surgical residents in my program."

—Dr. Matthew McGirt, Vanderbilt University Medical Center Assistant Professor of Neurological Surgery; Director of Clinical Spine Research

Dedication

This book is dedicated to our clients across the globe. Thank you for sharing your dreams with us. We are honored to serve your families and humbled by the confidence and trust you have placed in us.

We also want to express our appreciation to our vast editorial board:

Financial Analysts, Researchers, and Contributors
Todd DeKruyter, Rick Frith, Tim Beldner, Jake Whipp, Tony Ferrara, Chris Clark, Lauren Law, Colin Wiens, Scott Miller, Darin Archbold, Josh Nix, Randy Larson, Matt Lessman, BJ Carson, Scott Krafft, Bob Rachlow, Andy Parker, Andy Baker, Cameron Heasley, Forrest Friedow, Danelle Tainter, Andy Minnich, Justin Lance, Jacob Stevenson, Josh Jerele, Hannah Stroup, and Sam Hockley

Academic Advisor
Dr. John Grable, Chair of the Financial Planning Institute at Kansas State University
Online at www.ipfp.k-state.edu

Editors
Connie Anderson, Words & Deeds, Inc.
Online at www.WordsandDeedsInc.com

Danielle M. Smith
Contact, daniellemarlaine@gmail.com

Sara Israel, Larson Financial Group, LLC

Employee Benefit Consultants
Lee Warner & Jennifer Geci, The Warner Companies
Online at www.lwarner.com

Cover Design and Graphics
Alan Pranke, AMP 13
Online at www.amp13.com

Executive Coaches
Ken Doyle
Online at www.gettingresultscoaching.com

Joe Lukacs
Online at www.ipginc.net

Tax Review
Eric Meyer, MedTax, Inc.
Online at www.Medtax.com

Art Jensen, The Warner Companies
Online at www.lwarner.com

Legal Review
Randy Larson, J.D. and Greg Standeford, J.D., Larson Law Firm
Online at www.RSLLawFirm.com

Adam O. Kirwan, J.D., LL.M., The Kirwan Law Firm
Online at www.kirwanlawfirm.com

Additional thanks to our wives: Rachel, Rebecca, and Kim, and to our family, friends, and mentors who helped make this possible: (in no particular order) Kathy and Bob Beatty, Ryan and Becky Vickery, John and Annie Cowan, Rick and Cathy Hawks, Brian and Lani Mullis, Kevin and Angela Stockmaster, Matt and Laura McGirt, Michael Lim and Mary Shue, Doug and Jen Nuckols, Larry and Joy Martin, Rick and Penney Phillips, David and Sally Norton, Tom and Roberta Dougherty, Norman and Nancy Hockley, Aaron and Kristin Spalding, Derek and Kristin Seiler, and Ryland and Jennifer Scott.

LETTER FROM PAUL LARSON

Founder and CEO of Larson Financial Group

Isn't it perplexing that physicians receive so little financial and business education during their professional training? Attending physicians have told us that there just isn't enough time or expertise to focus on the business aspect of medicine during the training years. Thus physicians and their families are cast into the wild to learn these important lessons the hard way. Back in 2002 I was referred to my first physician client. He was in his late 40s, had been earning more than $500,000 per year for the last decade, and still had a net worth similar to a medical resident. After I overcame my initial shock, I set out to uncover how this had transpired. It was through this research that I came to the conclusion that there is little middle ground for older physicians. By the time they reach their late 50's, they are very well off, or are still struggling just as much to figure things out as they were during med school.

It was through this accidental discovery that Larson Financial Group–The Physician's Specialist™ was born. Each of our advisors at Larson Financial Group has a different story behind why they devote their practice to working with physicians.

My favorite story is about one of our advisors who fell into our specialty quite by chance. He was referred to two physicians working for the same ENT group. Each had an annual income of approximately $750,000. One lived off $350,000, gave away significant money, and had a great quality of life. The other was the complete opposite. With the same income, he spent $900,000 per year, and was up to his eyeballs in debt. Every time this client walked into the office, our advisor could sense the stress level growing, burdening the doctor like he had an elephant on his shoulders.

What intrigued our advisor most was that during residency, both of these professionals had believed they would be financially independent within five years of reaching a yearly income of $750,000. Both also admitted that they wished they had a trusted advisor to work with sooner because dealing with their financial life was taking too much time away from their families. This confirmed for our advisor that there was a gaping hole as it relates to sound financial advice for doctors, and motivated him to pursue this area of expertise.

All of our advisors at Larson Financial Group, whether they hold MBAs, JDs, CFPs, CFAs, or CPAs, have similar stories. They all found their passion and skill set uniquely suited to focus their energies on physicians. As a result, our firm is blessed today to help thousands of doctors and dentists across the country, including top professionals in almost every medical specialty, grow and protect their wealth. The doctors and families we serve represent what we enjoy most about the world of wealth planning: The opportunity to build meaningful, long-term relationships where we can help people achieve their most important dreams, and encourage them to accomplish great things.

In addition to providing a financial foundation for these medical professionals, we also assist many of our clients in more significant ways: Helping them with various aspects of adopting children, identifying the right mortgage for their dream homes, assisting them in contract negotiations, and helping them consider their long-term legacy.

> **As a result, our firm is now the largest in the country exclusively meeting the needs of doctors.**

Because of this, we are better equipped to deal with the financial challenges of practicing physicians than any other financial practice we know of in the world because it is all we do every day. We liken our business model to the medical profession. None of us would visit our family physician for open-heart surgery. In the same manner, our practice is distinctively specialized.

Our typical clients are physicians who have seen great success at an early age, but have found they do not have as much time to spend with family and friends as desired. Therefore, they are looking for ways to simplify their lives by handing off necessary but tedious responsibilities, like financial management. This provides them the opportunity to spend more time focusing on their passions – typically research, family, hobbies, and the churches or charities they support.

All in all, our clients represent the newest generation of medical leadership in our society. They are bright, family-oriented, sometimes workaholics, who have decided it is best to entrust our advisors to keep a

"All in all, our clients represent the newest generation of medical leadership in our society."

watchful eye on the big picture of their financial lives, rather than trying to do it all themselves.

Creating a Wealth Plan

As wealth managers, we are committed to serving as our clients' "financial quarterback." More than anything else, our job is to make sure their financial decisions are all "running the same play," and that "the play" is based on the core values and objectives they have established for their lives. Our clients serve as our head coach and set the direction of the game; our job is simply to call the plays and manage the team to make sure that the game is won, and opportunities are not missed.

We do this by crafting a financial plan that is custom designed for each of our client's individual circumstances. We look at their objectives and seek to ensure that their financial decisions are effectively moving them closer to achieving their dreams and goals, while keeping in mind their specified core values.

For our primary services and advice, we charge a reasonable, quarterly fee. Physicians appreciate this approach because it reminds them that our recommendations have their best interest front and center. This is not something we take lightly.

> By constantly listening to our clients we have built a highly specialized niche practice that takes the financial lives of our doctors to the next level.

What does it mean to have a fiduciary working for you?
At Larson Financial Group, we have always taken the stand that we will act as a fiduciary, whether the statutes require it or not. The financial industry is currently engaged in a heated battle with regard to holding

advisors to this fiduciary standard. In other words, many financial firms are not currently required by law to do what is best for their clients. What a sad and unnecessary debate! You have my personal commitment that our firm will do the right thing, whether or not the law requires it.

Black's Law Dictionary describes a fiduciary relationship as "one founded on trust or confidence reposed by one person in the integrity and fidelity of another." [1] A fiduciary has a duty to act on whatever he or she believes will best benefit the client's financial life. The financial planner/fiduciary is held to a standard of conduct and trust above that of a stranger, or a casual businessperson. The fiduciary must avoid "self-dealing" or "conflicts of interests" in which the potential benefit to the fiduciary is in conflict with what is best for the client. This is not true for stockbrokers, insurance agents, or bankers who are not usually held to the same fiduciary standard.

Why This Book?

Doctor's Eyes Only[TM][1] is meant to fill the void that was left in your medical training. It was written primarily to focus on topics for physicians that are within their first 12 years of practice or near to graduation from residency. Because every family has a different set of variables at play, there are no cookie-cutter solutions. This book is not meant to be the answer to all of your financial questions. Instead, it is designed to point you in the right direction, and better equip you to work with your team of professional advisors.

Ultimately, a primary mission of our practice is to help doctors and dentists become more educated decision makers. We hope this book will be a launching pad for you in this respect.

Please do not hesitate to contact us with any questions that arise from your reading. We would be honored to serve you and your family.

Kindest Regards,

Paul D. Larson, CFP®
CEO and Founder of Larson Financial Group

---

[1] *Doctor's Eyes Only*™ is a trademark owned by Doctor's Eyes Only Publishing, LLC. Used with permission. All rights reserved.

Table of Contents

Chapter 4: Investment Management

Stop Giving Away Your Growth

Basic Investment Terminology
Investment Accounts
    Tax-Deferred Accounts
    Tax-Free and Tax-Advantaged Accounts
    Taxable Accounts
    Annuities
Investment Options
    The Market
    Practice Ownership
    Real Estate
    Exotic / Private Opportunities
Market Investment Strategy
    Investment Growth and Reduced Volatility
    Investment Selection
    Market Timing / Forecasting
    Proper Diversification
    Investment Expenses
    Investment Taxes
    Investor Emotion and Overconfidence

Chapter 5: Education Planning

Avoid the Normal Errors Parents Make

How Much Should Be Funded?
Where to Save for College
Entitlement Concerns
Investing for College

Chapter 6: Tax Planning

Stop Giving the IRS 60% of Your Income

Tax Basics
Tax Strategy
    Reducing Taxable Income
    Reducing Taxes Owed
Alternative Minimum Tax
Uncommon Tax Strategies

Chapter 7: Estate Planning
Create a Legacy and Disinherit the IRS.

Values-Based Estate Planning Basics
    Wills
    A Trust for Your Children's Benefit
    Advanced Directives
    Powers of Attorney
The Financial Impact of Estate Planning
Flexible Estate Planning Strategies for Younger Families
    Testamentary Trusts
    Revocable Living Trusts
    Credit Shelter Trusts
    Disclaimer Provisions in Wills
    Irrevocable Life Insurance Trusts (ILITs)
    529 Plans
    UTMA Accounts
Multi-Generational Planning
Non-Citizen Spouses
Community Property States

Chapter 8: Asset Protection Planning
Beat a Lawsuit Before it Begins.

Asset Protection Defined
The Anatomy of a Lawsuit
What Asset Protection is Not
Asset Protection Strategies
    Insurance
    Exempt Assets
    Ownership Arrangements
    Un-bundling of Assets
    Equity Stripping
    Keeping a Low Profile

Chapter 9: Practice Management

Become a Successful Practitioner and Business Leader

Practice Leadership
Long-Term Vision
The Right People
Communication
Strategic and Tactical Time
Profit Maximization

Chapter 10: Employee Benefit Plans

Build an Efficient Benefits Structure

Benefits and Employee Compensation - Employer Perspective
  Common Challenges
Group Retirement Plans
Core Benefits
  Group Health Insurance
  Group Disability Insurance
  Group Long-Term Care Insurance
  Group Life Insurance
Voluntary Benefits
  Dependent Care Reimbursement Arrangements
  Portable Disability Insurance for Residents
  Guaranteed Group Life Insurance
Executive Benefits and Golden Handcuffs

Wrap Up

Choose Your Team Wisely to Make Success a Reality

Questions to Ask Before Hiring a Financial Advisor
About the Authors
Works Cited

The Missing Course

Why Physicians Look Rich but Feel Poor

One of our most memorable client moments came when a physician was self-deprecating enough to make the following statement:

"Do you know what MD stands for?" he asked. "Money Dumb! Do you know why? Because in 15 years of post-high school training, I haven't had one class in economics, finance, budgeting, contract negotiations, or business, and yet, now I'm supposed to be an expert in all of these!"

We can think of no other field where a professional is expected to manage so many variables for which they have received so little training. *Doctor's Eyes Only*™ is meant to serve as a supplemental curriculum that covers the bare essentials necessary to properly manage these aspects for your practice and family. Without this solid understanding, you are more likely to end up like many of the physicians we encounter at the later stages of their career: owning lots of stuff, but lacking true assets.

This book is designed to help you save or recapture millions of dollars over your lifetime, but we would be remiss to not first acknowledge that at best, money is only a very small part of true wealth. Israel's King Solomon may have been the wealthiest man to ever live. In his excellent book, *The Richest Man Who Ever Lived*, Steven K. Scott shares that King Solomon's gold alone was estimated to be worth hundreds of billions of dollars. During his rule from around 970 to 930 BC, Solomon amassed wealth estimated to be many times greater than that of any of the world's wealthiest technology oracles today. [2] Reflecting on his massive fortune in the later years of his life, Solomon poignantly summarized the same emotional challenges that we often see physicians facing after finally building substantial income and/or assets at a relatively young age:

I also tried to find meaning by building huge homes for myself and by planting beautiful vineyards. I made gardens and parks, filling them with all kinds of fruit trees... I also owned large herds and flocks, more than any of the kings who had lived in Jerusalem before me. I collected great sums of silver and gold, the treasure of many kings and provinces... and had many beautiful concubines. I had everything a man could desire!

So I became greater than all who had lived in Jerusalem before me, and my wisdom never failed me. Anything I wanted, I would take. I denied myself no pleasure... But as I looked at everything I had worked so hard to accomplish, it was all so meaningless–like chasing the wind. There was nothing really worthwhile anywhere. (Ecclesiastes 2:4-11) [3]

Solomon achieved the modern-day American Dream. He was financially independent and had *everything* he could ever want in the form of material possessions. Yet he realized that this material wealth, *on its own,* was all meaningless–like trying to chase after the wind. Solomon further explained his realizations about false success in a later passage:

Those who love money will never have enough. How meaningless to think that wealth brings true happiness! The more you have, the more people come to help you spend it. So what good is wealth– except perhaps to watch it slip through your fingers! People who work hard sleep well, whether they eat little or much. But the rich seldom get a good night's sleep. (Ecclesiastes 5:10-12) [3]

Solomon eloquently emphasized that wealth is not a sure path to happiness. Consider that although physicians rank in the top 1% of wage earners in the United States, their marriages are often less happy than the general population. Many families have learned the hard way that wealth does not lead to automatic happiness in all facets of life–including marriage. Conversely, wealth can actually be a root cause of incredible family tension if not put in proper perspective.

Wayne and Mary Sotile discuss this phenomenon poignantly in their book, *The Medical Marriage:* [4]

Contemporary medical couples rank among the most stressed and surprised segment of the married population.

They also share the words of a specialist, who made the following inquiry,

I'm a 'rich doctor,' right? So why do I lie awake nights trying to figure out how we can keep this lifestyle of ours afloat on less money? It costs more than we ever expected.

Visit www.DoctorsEyesOnly.com for additional marriage resources, and a podcast exclusively for physicians and their spouses.

Finance-related tension is not exclusive to marriage; it can trickle into other relationships as well. Take for example the physician and his sister who no longer speak to each other because he wanted to keep their dad's farm and she wanted to sell it for cash after he passed. Or the business partners who spent years working together for peanuts to build a multimillion-dollar specialty practice. All of that work only to have their relationship torn apart when the money finally started pouring in, and they could not amicably agree on how to divide the profits.

The simple truth is that most things in life are more important than obtaining wealth. The most fulfilled physicians we know use money as a tool, but they never allow money to become the *focus* of their life or family. Although they are often capable of managing the ins and outs of their financial lives, many times they delegate these responsibilities to trusted advisors. This provides them with the opportunity to devote their time, efforts, and energy to areas that are more important: their family, their careers, their hobbies, their faith, and so forth.

Though delegating their financial life to a professional is not the ideal solution for every doctor, we would suggest that unless you absolutely enjoy financial planning *and* you are willing to make a *daily* commitment to continued financial education, your family will certainly miss out on maximizing its full financial potential.

"Those who love money will never have enough. How meaningless to think that wealth brings true happiness! The more you have, the more people come to help you spend it." [3] – King Solomon

Most doctors do not want to spend time each day dealing with their financial lives; instead, they want their family's finances to be *less* of a focus. If you are part of this group, you would be much better off hiring advisors whose sole mission is to ensure that your family takes advantage of the many strategic financial planning opportunities available.

This often prompts a great question: How can you know which advisors to trust with your financial future? Let's face it, these days everyone claims to be a "financial planner"–your banker, your auto insurance agent, your stockbroker, and the guy who sells insurance down the street. Shocking as it may sound to a physician, in the financial world, the CFP®[2] and CFA board exams are totally *optional* for advisors, and few advisors ever take either of them. This is the financial industry's equivalent of a family medicine physician listing himself as a neurosurgeon. This would not be permissible in the medical world, but in the financial sector, this misclassification of advisors is all too prevalent.

When it comes to your family's financial health, it is important that you place your trust in someone who is actually trustworthy. By understanding the right questions to ask, you'll have a better chance at making that decision. It is for this reason that we provide you with a series of questions to ask any advisor you have hired or are contemplating hiring. This list begins on page 212 at the back of the book and is a great tool for evaluating your current advisor(s) or identifying a reputable new one.

Building a Financial Plan

Most physicians' lost financial potential is not caused primarily by poor investment choices. Rather, it is a lack of coordination across all areas

---

[2] CFP is a registered trademark of the Certified Financial Planner Board of Standards, Inc.

of their financial lives that cause most doctors to give up their greatest potential. This book distinguishes ten important planning areas that every doctor must address in order to build and implement a properly balanced and coordinated financial plan.

Areas to Address in a Coordinated Financial Plan

Cash Flow	Tax Planning
Risk Management	Estate Planning
Debt	Asset Protection
Retirement	Practice Management
Education	Employee Benefit Plans

Although we have done our best to make *Doctor's Eyes Only*™ usable as a reference manual, the real money is made or lost by knowing how to correctly put all of the various pieces together. A good financial advisor specializes in helping you put each of these pieces together into one comprehensive and well-managed plan. Physicians often demonstrate that this coordination can mean the difference between hundreds of thousands–to millions–of dollars of additional wealth over their lifetimes.

Take for example many doctors and dentists who have a large balance in their 401(k) or 403(b) plan through their practice. It astounds us that many of these investors have no idea that along with their account balance, their *tax burden* is also *compounding* throughout their working years. Without coordinating their future tax situation with their investment decisions today, they could face disaster when they reach their retirement years.

We liken this financial coordination to a big jigsaw puzzle. If just one piece of the puzzle is missing, everything else becomes distorted.

This book's ten chapters cover each of the important areas of your financial life. While each chapter can stand alone, it is vital that your financial plan addresses all of them in a coordinated fashion. This is exactly what a Financial Advisor who works exclusively with physicians has been specifically trained to do.

In Summary

The goal of this introduction is to help you realize that you can go in one of two directions with your family's financial future.

1. You can devote a significant amount of your time on a regular basis to stay abreast of financial issues, and continue to manage your family's financial playbook on your own. If you follow this path, do so with extreme caution. Physicians face a "crisis of overconfidence" as it relates to their own financial abilities. Consistent studies document that the more confidence a physician has in his or her own financial expertise, the less likely he or she is to actually be correct in this assessment. [5] [6] Stop taking financial advice from your colleagues. The odds are that this advice will not be right for your unique situation.

2. Alternatively, you can delegate this work to a specialized professional so that you can spend your time following your passions, rather than worrying about how to finance them.

At the end of the day, our hope is that every physician is being properly served when it comes to his or her financial life–either through his or her own efforts, or through those of an advisor or team of advisors. We want your financial life to be an area of peace for your family, not a source of stress. That outcome will only occur when your financial decisions are properly aligned with the core values you share for your family, and when each piece of your financial life is working together in harmony with all of the other pieces.

If this book helps to move your family closer to this outcome, we will have accomplished our most important objective.

CHAPTER 1

Cash Flow

Keep $3,000,000
and Regain Peace of Mind

"The things you own end up owning you."
Tyler Durden
Main character from the movie Fight Club [7]

At an educational workshop we hosted for resident physicians at a prestigious institution, a final-year resident remarked, "I was so glad to have signed a contract with a practice two years before graduating. They have been paying me $2,000 per month as a forgivable loan during my last year of training. That gave me enough extra cash to lease a car for $970 per month during residency."

This physician got to his new practice, and quickly learned that the partners expected him to work 90 hours per week, and take the majority of the call time required of their group–things they had previously failed to mention. His family made the decision to move on to another practice, but the forgivable loan had to be paid back to the group in full.

The most basic foundational requirement to a successful financial life is learning how to manage your cash flow and live well within your means. The way you spend your money influences all other areas of your life. Without a plan for managing income, most physicians waste more than $3 million in poor spending, investment, and home-buying decisions, etc. Without a plan, money will inevitably find a way to leave faster than it arrives. An ancient prophet once proclaimed,

Look at what is happening to you! You have planted much but harvest little. You eat but you are not satisfied... Your wages disappear as though you were putting them in pockets filled with holes! (Haggai 1:5) [3]

It is imperative that you have a plan for your income. Without a plan, physicians rarely develop the habits necessary to keep their hard-earned income in their own pockets.

The Phases of Income and Wealth Building

The habits needed for successful money management differ at various stages of your practice. As you progress in your practice, three distinct phases of life will all create different cash-flow management opportunities and challenges that require the establishment of new habits.

Phase I: The Lean Years–Survival

Phase II: Disposable Income–Success

Phase III: Meaningful Wealth–Significance

Phase I: The Lean Years–Survival

Phase I begins upon completion of medical residency or dental school. At this point, student loans are usually at their peak, and unless a spouse was working or parents were helping financially, credit cards are often part of the equation. Bottom line: Very little cash is set aside in savings and investments.

This is normal. Cash flow was probably very tight prior to graduation. At this point, the goal is not so much to accumulate massive wealth as it is to begin building solid financial habits that will persist throughout your lifetime.

Phase II: Disposable Income–Success

Phase II begins once the high-interest consumer debt is finally paid back, and you have had the opportunity to build up some emergency reserves. The point of entry into Phase II is often the most critical phase on the road to wealth for a young family. *It is at this crucial juncture that families must decide how to handle their newly acquired cash flow.* If this conscious decision is never made, most families generally default to spending every dime of additional income, and do not save enough for the future.

Before reaching Phase II, it may seem absurd that someone could actually spend ten times as much income from one year to the next. However, our experience proves that Solomon's wisdom is true: *Expenses, by default, rise to meet income.* The goal throughout the Disposable Income Phase is to avoid the "default" experience, and to ensure that your cash flow pattern allows for saving a meaningful portion of your much-increased income on a regular basis.

Phase III: Meaningful Wealth–Significance

Phase III begins as financially successful physicians accumulate assets of $1 million or more.

> **At this point, the family has the opportunity (and often the responsibility) to move their financial stature from a position of success to a position of true significance.**

With good planning, these physicians have the ability to make a meaningful societal impact by leveraging their time, talents, and treasures to the causes they are most passionate about. The financial planning required at this stage of the game becomes more advanced, but it also greatly impacts the bottom line of the family's net worth.

Spenders vs. Savers

During these phases of life, we believe DNA and family upbringing both have a lot to do with the financial habits that are developed.

The size of income does not matter if spending always exceeds it. This may seem obvious, but we regularly encounter doctors who struggle with this; they always seem to live just a step ahead of their income. Nothing will get a family into bigger financial trouble more quickly than the propensity to consume more than they earn. Remember the words of King Solomon from the Introduction, "Those who love money will never have enough."[3]

The financial issues we face today are the same ones prominent citizens have struggled with for millennia. It may seem ridiculous that an athlete or entertainer earning millions of dollars per year would ever go bankrupt, but this happens on a regular basis. Kim Basinger, P.T. Barnum, Mark Twain, Oscar Wilde, Donald Trump, Tony Gwynn, Jerry Lee Lewis, MC Hammer, Henry Ford, Burt Reynolds, and Walt Disney are just a small sampling of celebrities and icons that have gone through financial hardship. [8]

Through countless appointments with our clients, we have learned firsthand that people are either hard-wired as "savers" or as "spenders." Saving comes easily to some people, and others must work very hard at it.

Savers would never dream of spending more than they earn. They naturally pinch pennies and regularly set money aside. While saving money is a great thing, savers can also tend to be too restrictive. For example, one doctor we worked with drew a comfortable seven-figure salary, yet he still lectured his wife on buying brand-name pickles from a grocery store. Another doctor did not buy fruit if the price was above a certain dollar per pound. He was the same way with hamburger. His daughter actually grew up thinking she was poor because there were weeks when they "couldn't afford" to buy hamburger. In reality, they had millions of dollars in the bank.

Although these are extreme cases, it is common to see the family or spouse of a saver stressed out because they rarely get to enjoy the fruits of the breadwinner's hard work.

Spenders, on the other hand, are no strangers to instant gratification. If they see something they want, they find a way to justify purchasing it. Prioritizing how money is spent (or not spent) rarely enters their thoughts. This can lead to financial disaster as savings and investments fail to accumulate and debt piles up instead. One young client came to us after purchasing a $950,000 home, a new luxury car, and a speedboat, only to realize he did not have enough extra cash flow to pay for his daughter's school tuition. He was devastated by this, and realized he needed help managing his family's financial affairs.

Fortunately, it seems that most families consist of one saver and one spender, which results in a more balanced financial life. However, exceptions are possible, with the biggest financial challenges often occurring for those couples with two spenders and no savers. The problem: Most spenders do not realize how little control they truly have over their spending. This usually makes for financial setback unless special checks and balances are put in place to protect the family. The good news is that by introducing good financial habits into the mix, they can usually get their overspending in check.

Developing Sound Financial Habits

Whether a saver or a spender, it is important to develop sound financial habits in order to better manage your monthly cash flow. We believe that no matter the financial phase, every physician should practice these four financial habits.

Financial Habits for Cash Flow Management:
Habit #1: Maintain Emergency / Opportunity Reserves
Habit #2: Categorize Your Life—Build a Budget
Habit #3: Give to Causes Greater than Yourself
Habit #4: Begin on the Final Page

Habit #1: Maintain Emergency / Opportunity Reserves

Life changes quickly, and the unexpected frequently occurs. Financial planning textbooks often suggest that you should set aside cash equal to six months worth of your income.[9] The reality is that many doctors and dentists do not keep that much in reserves. Rather, most of our physicians maintain about two to three months worth of monthly living expenses in a checking account or money market fund. For additional emergency reserves, they rely on a home equity line of credit, four-day access to their investment funds, and/or an unsecured line of credit.

> **The first key to a long-term successful financial life is access to adequate resources for emergencies or opportunities.**

Habit #2: Categorize Your Life–Build a Budget

In addition to building adequate emergency reserves, we also recommend doctors separate their financial responsibilities into five main categories in order to help build a basic budget for their financial lives:

1. Giving
2. Saving
3. Living
4. Debt Reduction
5. Taxes

Each category should be assigned a percentage of the total income. Provided that the percentages are properly balanced, this can make life much easier.

Doctors and dentists often wonder how they should go about establishing the above percentages. Every situation is different, but we offer the reader some basic guidelines in Habit #3 and Habit #4.

Habit #3: Give to Causes Greater than Yourself

At first we were surprised when our clients asked us about how much money they should be giving away. We had not expected to be involved in such a personal decision. It turns out that many physicians have questions about giving money to charity or tithing to their place of worship. This is exciting. It tells us that we are involved with a generous portion of society that believes financial success is not something to be taken for granted.

On the surface this issue is personal, but we believe the question arises as many people share a worldview that this life is about more than just ourselves.

As authors, we personally approach life from a Christian worldview, and this influences the way we manage the financial resources that have been entrusted to each of us. The world's major religious faiths share three fundamental financial principles as it relates to giving, that are paramount to this discussion:

1. Those of us who have resources also have a responsibility to help provide for those who do not.
2. Giving to those less fortunate should involve a measure of personal sacrifice or we are not doing our part.
3. Giving should be done at all phases of life. (We are fooling ourselves by thinking that we will give later when we have more resources.)

In his highly recommended book, *The Treasure Principle,* Randy Alcorn sums up these teachings with the great reminder, "You can't take it with you when you go." [10]

Money is a temporary tool for a temporary life. At the end of the day, we know of no man or woman who hopes his or her gravestone says, "Here lies a really rich doctor." Instead, our hope is that we can help our clients achieve enough peace of mind regarding their own financial lives that it frees them to devote more of their time, effort, and energy to building a meaningful legacy.

If your primary question is, "How much *should* we give?" perhaps a paradigm shift in your thinking is appropriate. A better question might be, "How much *can* we give?" In their book *Why Good Things Happen to Good People*, Stephen Post, Ph.D. and Jill Neimark, document consistent studies that show those who are generous with their time and wealth are happier, healthier, less stressed, live longer, and feel more spiritually fulfilled. [11] Therefore, when it comes to cash flow management, we believe one of the most important habits to establish early on is a consistent method of giving away a portion of your resources to passions greater than yourself.

Dr. Ryan Vickery, a successful anesthesiologist, summed up these principles well for us in a personal interview. He found that perspective is vital in understanding why it makes so much sense to give away time or resources,

> *"For years," he said, "I focused the actions of each day on the short term. It was as if the only important part of life was the next 3-5 days."*

He then added, "When we actually sat down on different occasions to give it some real thought, it connected for my wife, Becky, and me that life is really about something much bigger than what we were previously focused on." [12]

When we look at life in terms of the "big picture," as shown above, whether we believe in eternity or not, everything else will change. If we focus on the long-term, the way we interact with our spouses will change, the way we parent our children will change, and most important, as it relates to this book, the way we manage our financial lives must change.

Dr. Ben Carson, director of the pediatric neurosurgery division at Johns Hopkins says the following in his book, *The Big Picture: Getting Perspective on What's Really Important in Life*: [13]

The reason we need to consider our priorities carefully–and the principles on which we base them–is that they impact every important choice we make in life. Those choices further determine both the ultimate direction of our lives and the unique set of opportunities that will come our way.

How is a doctor to make this long-term perspective on priorities practical in his or her own financial life? For those physicians who have not yet established their own philosophy for their family's charitable giving, we offer a suggestion. Our approach is simple. Begin giving away a set percentage of the after-tax paycheck you bring home. To begin, the percentage is irrelevant unless your religious beliefs dictate otherwise. Just do something to get started. Make it a goal as a family to increase this percentage whenever possible, but at least every year. Even if you only increase by 0.5% per year, you will still be giving more and more, and likely finding your efforts increasingly more fulfilling.

Note: *It turns out that we benefit most when we connect face to face with those whom we support, and we are most fulfilled about giving when we are on a first-name basis with those who receive our gifts. (14) This is a topic that will be explored further in our upcoming book on building a lasting legacy.*

Giving becomes easier once it develops into a regular habit. We have yet to meet a physician who started giving and later regretted it. You need not take our word for this, instead consider the words of Dr. Will Mayo:

By 1894 my brother and I had paid for our homes. Our clinic was on its feet. Patients kept coming. Our theories seemed to be working out. The mortality rate among our cases was satisfyingly low. Money began to pile up. To us it seemed to be more money than any two men had any right to have. We talked it over a lot, that year of 1894 we came to a decision. That year we put aside half of our income. We couldn't touch a cent of that half for ourselves...

From 1894 onward we have never used more than half of our incomes on ourselves and our families... My brother and I have both put ourselves on salaries now. The salaries are far less than half our incomes. We live within them...

My interest and my brother's interest is to train men for the service of humanity. What can I do with one pair of hands? But, if I can train 50 or 500 pairs of hands, I have helped hand on the torch." (15)

Habit #4: Begin on the Final Page
Simply building emergency reserves, categorizing your life, and giving to great causes will not automatically lead to financial success. The remaining key is to spend the right amount less than you earn. In order to determine the right amount to properly set aside for the future, you must first "begin on the final page." This is an important recurring theme from the *Doctor's Eyes Only*™ podcast (subscribe online at *www. DoctorsEyesOnly.com*). The point is simple: if you don't know where you're headed; there is no good way to get there. Instead, when you know what you want to achieve, you can work backward to determine the amount that you need to save today in order to make it happen.

Delayed gratification is a difficult concept for many Americans to grasp. We live in a society that thrives on getting whatever we want whenever we want it. Fortunately, doctors have a much better understanding of delayed gratification than the general public, or they never would have spent so much time in training. No different than setting your sights on becoming a physician, it is crucial to set some reasonable objectives about what you want to achieve in the future as it relates to your financial life.

> **By beginning on the final page, and knowing what you want to accomplish tomorrow, it is possible to determine the sacrifice that must be made today.**

Doctors and dentists are often pleasantly surprised when they find out that they can still enjoy a great lifestyle today, while at the same time providing for the future. In fact, families tell us it is comforting to know the appropriate amount they need to save, to set aside for the future. By knowing that, they also know how much they can spend and enjoy today.

It is always better to know sooner, rather than later, if your expectations are realistic. When it comes to money, almost everyone hates surprises.

Creating a Savings Target

We are often asked: "How much should we be saving for the future?" Because each family's situation has so many different variables, there are no generic answers to this question. However, the following chart, from the *Journal of Financial Planning*, provides some general guidelines based on the most common situations we see for younger physicians.[3]

---

[3] "Comfortable retirement" seeks to replace 50% of pre-retirement income. This data is provided through a source we believe to be fully reliable but we cannot directly attest to the accuracy of the findings. Data is based on historical findings and does not guarantee future results.

Approximate Savings Amounts Required from Gross Income to Achieve a Comfortable Retirement		
	30 years of withdrawals	40 years of withdrawals
20 years to accumulate	≈36%	≈39%
30 years to accumulate	≈17%	≈19%

Notice that achieving a comfortable retirement requires a far larger portion of your income to provide for retirement than the typical 10% you may have previously heard. Of course, the earlier you begin saving, the lower the percentage of income required to meet your goals. Note that this issue is a gigantic aspect of what makes your financial life so unique as a physician. If you had 40 years to save for retirement, your required savings rate might drop to as low as 8% of your income. Because physicians typically desire a much shorter time frame to reach financial independence, this dictates their savings rate must be greatly increased.[16]

The issue of *where* you save your money (what type of accounts, investments, etc. that you use) is also critical and is discussed in more detail in the Investment Management section, beginning on page 56. The lifestyle you desire in retirement is also paramount in making your decisions.

Recent Example

John became a partner with his orthopedic group, giving him an annual income increase of $200,000. It was important to him and his wife, Becca, to establish strong financial habits for their future. They wanted to know they were saving enough money to provide for their children's education and their own retirement, but they also wanted to eliminate their debts, and make sure they were regularly donating to their favorite causes.

They established the following plan for each paycheck:
- *The first 12% would be given away*
- *Another 18% would go toward saving and investing*
- *60% would go for living expenses (including the minimum debt payment allowed)*

• *The remaining 10% would be applied as additional payments to eliminate their debt earlier than scheduled, and this 10% would be used to increase their savings percentage, once the debts had been fully eliminated.*

The basic budget shown above was the catalyst that helped John and Becca feel comfortable spending their "living" money because they had already provided for everything else. For the first time ever, they felt like they could go on a great family vacation without feeling guilty about their large mortgage payment.

PRACTICAL APPLICATION

Having a plan and purpose for your income is fundamental to all other financial decisions. The first step is to spend some time dreaming about what you want the "final page" to look like.

• What type of retirement lifestyle do you genuinely want to enjoy?
• Is it important to you to be in a position to help your children attend college? Grad school? Does it matter if it is public or private education?
• Do you want to leave other money to your loved ones? If so, how much, and for what purposes?
• Are there causes that you find important enough that you would like to see them attached to the legacy you leave for your great-grandchildren?
• Are there other dreams you have that would require financial resources? What are they?
• In order for you to feel like you have made exceptional progress in your financial life, what needs to happen over the next three years?

The next step is to prioritize the four opportunities for your money (mark 1–4 to designate your highest to lowest priority items, with taxes #5):

___ Living   ___ Debt Reduction
___ Giving   _5_ Taxes
___ Saving and Investing

Now that you have prioritized them, take your order of priority and move it below. Next, designate the percent of your after-tax income (net income) that you plan to send to each category.

Note: Most physicians do not have a great handle on what percentages are required for each of these items. Helping you properly determine these answers is a big part of a financial advisor's value proposition.

Top Priority _____
% Dedicated _____

Second Priority _____
% Dedicated _____

Third Priority _____
% Dedicated _____

Fourth Priority _____
% Dedicated _____

Now that you have developed a plan for your income, implement it by taking the funds needed for giving, debt reduction, and saving and investment right off of the top of all income you earn. The best way to keep this money separate is to automatically deposit it into an account that does not commingle with your normal living expenses. All other dollars can be used for living expenses however you choose.

For further reading:
- *The Richest Man Who Ever Lived,* by Steven K. Scott
- *The Medical Marriage,* by Wayne and Mary Sotile
- *The Treasure Principle*, by Randy Alcorn
- *Why Good Things Happen to Good People*, Stephen Post, Ph.D. and Jill Neimark
- *The Big Picture*, Dr. Ben Carson

CHAPTER 2

Debt Management
Get the Monkey Off Your Back

"... the borrower is servant to the lender." (Proverbs 22:7) [3]

Cash flow and debt management are intimately linked facets of a successful financial life. Debt is incredibly powerful. It can be leveraged to provide opportunities that cash flow would never provide, such as a dream home, and it can also devastate families through the stress it causes when payments cannot be met. As such, debt is a tool that should always be used cautiously. If not, it can easily and quickly become a monkey that is impossible to get off of your back.

> **A fine line exists between debts that help your family, and debts that become your family's master.**

It is important to note that while paying off debt quickly is often a positive decision, it should be balanced with achieving your other financial goals. We would be concerned if clients devoted the next ten years of their life to paying off debt at the direct expense of setting aside any savings for the future. Because cash flow is a limited resource, it is imperative that your family makes a strategic decision when determining how much of your income to allocate toward debt reduction versus savings.

A general rule is that debt with an interest rate over 6 to 8% should often be eliminated *prior* to sending dollars to savings and investments.

The following pages become more detailed, and deal with different types of debt and solutions to common debt problems. If this is a non-issue, you may want to skip ahead to Chapter 3. Note that before you completely leave this issue you will want to check the discussion on mortgage deductibility beginning on page 31.

Consumer Debt

When we refer to consumer debt, we are referring to loans outside of mortgages and student loans. Of these loans, the most problematic are certainly credit cards. This is the ultimate monkey. We have encountered physicians with as many as twenty-three credit cards. People often assume that they should pay off the cards in order of the highest to lowest interest rates. Instead, we often suggest a different approach.

Rather than paying down the cards with the highest interest rates first, we often recommend that our clients focus on the cards that can be paid off the quickest.

Eliminating credit cards in this manner creates what we call the "snowball effect." You gain more and more momentum along the way, until all of your credit cards have been eliminated. This approach actually decreases the amount of interest being paid in many circumstances, and psychologically it works better because the progress is visible. A final key to success is to begin saving the funds that are no longer required for debt payments once the target debts are fully eliminated.

Often, an even better approach to credit card elimination is a consolidation loan. By reducing the debts from many to one, the debt can often become more manageable. As long as new habits are established in conjunction with this strategy, this may be the most practical route to reducing the stress surrounding debts.

As this book goes to press, the United States is still suffering through the economic aftereffects of the "great mortgage meltdown." Banks have tightened up lending and lines of credit, but some great resources are still available for doctors. Just remember, it is more important than ever to maintain a clean credit report.

Student Loans

Most young physicians have substantial student loans. Our record loan to date belonged to one young couple that had over $680,000 in combined student loans. Although these loans can feel like a heavy burden, if your education has led to the opportunity for substantially higher-than-average income in a career that you enjoy, it was a great decision.

The following chart shows the average indebtedness of survey respondents from the 2010 graduating class: [17]

Medical Student Education:
Costs, Debts, and Loan Repayment Facts

Graduation Indebtedness			
	Public	Private	All
Mean	$148,222	$172,422	$157,944
Median	$150,000	$180,000	$160,000

When we asked one young physician how he felt about his student loans (with only a 1.6% interest rate), he responded, *"They scare me to death!"* Because the detailed intricacies of exactly how to structure your individual student loans are beyond the scope of this book, we thought it important to point out the basics that every indebted doctor and dentist should know.

Student Loan Fundamentals:
- Consolidate your student loans to lock in the lowest possible interest rate and payment.
- If your interest rate is greater than 6 to 8%, and the government is not covering your interest while in deferment or forbearance, try your best to pay at least the interest each year so that it stops accumulating. Only do this *after* you have already established adequate emergency reserves (including any funds that may be needed for a down payment on a home).
- When you enter the repayment stage, give yourself the most flexibility possible by electing the longest repayment period available. This should not cause your interest rate to increase, and you are permitted to make extra payments if desired to pay off the loan sooner than required.
- You may benefit from consulting with a private banker to see if he or she can assist in consolidating your private loans to one new unsecured loan with a lower interest rate.

- Remember, provided that your student loans are in only your name, usually your spouse would not be contractually obligated to repay them if you die.

- Private student loans typically have a fluctuating interest rate that is relatively high, compared to other student loans in normal interest-rate conditions. These are usually the first student loans that should be repaid.

- Be careful not to commingle your student loans with non-student loans during a consolidation or buyout–at least during residency. Doing so would likely eliminate your ability to take a tax deduction on the loan interest that you pay.

"Be careful not to commingle your student loans with non-student loans during a consolidation or buyout."

Note: *This issue is usually no longer a factor upon graduation as your income should be too high to deduct the student loan interest anyway.*

Mortgages

Most physicians have four main questions regarding their mortgages:

1. How much home can we afford?
2. How much money should we put down?
3. How should we structure our mortgage?
4. Now that we have enough money, should we pay off our home, or keep our money invested instead?

An Affordable Home

To address the first issue, note that outside of divorce and lawsuits, little else can be as financially crippling to a physician as buying a home that is too expensive. Families in Phases I and II (see page 10) should avoid having a mortgage any larger than one to two times their annual income. However, this amount is considerably less than a lender will likely offer you for a mortgage. In other words, a bank's pre-approval does not always equal a wise financial decision.

For someone to claim they have an "affordable home," it should meet the following three criteria:

1. Your house payment should not prevent your family from doing the other things that are important to you and them.
2. You should be in a position to have your mortgage(s) completely paid off by the time you reach your desired financial independence age.
3. You should not have to worry about the impact future economic changes could have on your mortgage. For example, rising interest rates should not be a worry for you if your mortgage is structured properly, and a decrease in your Medicare reimbursement rate should not pose a major threat to your cash flow as a result of your mortgage, because to begin with, you did not purchase too much home.

Down Payment

With the mortgage market in such flux over the past couple of years, physicians are asking more and more, "How much money should we have for a down payment?" Our short answer is that this is the wrong question. It goes back to the affordability issues described above. Provided your home meets the criteria suggested, it should not matter whether you put 5% or 50% down.

The only caveat is you might receive a lower interest rate by putting more money down. Going this route might make sense at times, but this issue has to be addressed on a case-by-case basis by evaluating these elements: cash flow, emergency reserves, asset protection issues, return on other investments, psychological attitude toward debt, other debts, propensity for risk, and other variables. In other words, an advisor's advice is well warranted for this issue because it is more complex than simply acquiring a slightly lower mortgage rate.

Mortgage Structure

We want our clients to be in a position to pay off their mortgage by their desired financial independence age or earlier.

Families should consider the following course of action when determining the correct mortgage structure:

- Acquire a thirty-year amortized loan with a fixed interest rate that lasts for either seven to ten years, or the length of time you plan to remain in the home–whichever is greater.
- Structure your payments to remain small so that your cash flow is not all tied up by the mortgage, as long as you are saving enough extra to pay the home off by your desired financial independence age.
- Investigate financing options with mortgage bankers and brokers to determine the best loan pricing available. A financial advisor typically helps to manage this process on behalf of his or her clients.

The various mortgage experts we work with often recommend a seven- to ten-year Adjustable Rate Mortgage (ARM) to clients. This may be true *provided that you can acquire a meaningfully lower interest rate* than a traditional 30-year fixed loan would offer. The statistics show that few people ever keep a mortgage for longer than five to eight years. [18] They either move or refinance. By using a longer-term ARM, physicians can often save a lot of unnecessary interest payments over time.

> **Note:** *In the mortgage environment for the past few years, interest rates on 30-year fixed mortgages have sometimes been less than interest rates on adjustable rate mortgages. In this position, we would suggest using the fixed-rate mortgage, as there is no substantial benefit to accepting the potential added risk of the 7-10 year adjustable rate mortgage. Only use an ARM if the interest rate provides substantial interest savings for you.*

By coordinating the expertise of a good mortgage professional with that of your financial advisor, you can ensure your mortgage structure is in line with other financial objectives, and that it is properly coordinated with the current industry trends.[4]

---

[4] The most appropriate course of action for your personal mortgage situation should be evaluated by a professional who understands the big picture of your financial situation. No action should be taken based solely on the information provided in this book.

Banks or Brokers

Where you go to obtain your mortgage can greatly affect the products available to you and the expenses you will incur. Traditional banks and mortgage brokers are the two primary lending vendors.

In our experience, banks sometimes charge less in fees, but often offer higher interest rates than their broker counterparts. The key is to investigate both options to determine which will provide the best solution for your situation.

The mortgage market is dynamic, so it pays to look into all options. For example, a few great banks right now will provide 100% financing for doctors without requiring them to buy mortgage insurance or pay added fees.[5] This might be an attractive option if you have little to offer in the form of a down payment. If you are not aware of these options, you might end up choosing a more expensive 80/20 loan, paying extra for mortgage insurance, or even having to wait to buy a home until you can save up a large down payment.

Four large banks have recently requested assistance from our firm in developing mortgage programs exclusively for high-income medical professionals. Our hope is that they will listen and design additional programs that meet the needs of our clients, as this area is not competitive enough in the current marketplace.

Visit *www.LarsonFinancial.com/Mortgage* to learn about our latest mortgage options.

Paying Off Your Home

At the other end of the spectrum, many of our doctors are in a position where they could liquidate their investments and pay off their homes, if they so desired. They often ask what their best course of action is

---

[5] Not available in all areas due to declining market status or other reasons.

in this respect. Our answer: It is a function of three elements working closely together,
1. Economics
2. Psychology
3. Asset Protection

First, consider the economic component, as this is the easiest part. If you can earn a higher net return on your invested dollars than your mortgage is costing you (on a net-of-tax basis), why pay off the mortgage? This is especially true if you can accomplish this with little market risk involved. With our current 6% (or less) mortgage rates, an investor could be fairly conservative with his or her investments and still expect to earn a higher net rate of return. Change Mortgage to the mortgage interest deduction also helps. This tax relief enables a 6% mortgage rate to morph into a 3.6% *after-tax equivalent* interest rate for those who find themselves in the highest current income tax bracket.[6]

However, in addition to economics, we realize that psychology is always involved with debt. No client has suggested that they love debt, and wish they had as much of it as possible. Even though the economic and protection factors may suggest that maintaining a mortgage makes the most sense, if it will cause you to lose sleep, we suggest you pay it off.

Finally, because people can become so emotionally attached to their homes, asset protection must be considered in the decision-making process. We address this in more detail in the Asset Protection chapter beginning on page 141. Some states, like Iowa and Florida, provide unlimited asset protection for home equity, which makes it very difficult to lose your home in a lawsuit or bankruptcy in these states.[19] Along similar lines, Texas provides unlimited asset protection, but only if the property is less than one hundred acres.[7] What a great law that only Texas would have. [20]

However, other states like Missouri, Indiana, Michigan, Tennessee, Colorado, California, and Ohio provide very little protection of home equity. [20] [21] If you live in such a state, maintaining a mortgage can actually help reduce the risk of losing your property in the event of a

---

[6] At the time of publication, Congress continues to debate on cutting out the mortgage interest deduction for high-income earners. A change like this could have a large impact on the economics described above.

[7] 10 acres for urban areas, 100 acres for rural areas. [20]

lawsuit. Understanding how your state treats home equity, from an asset protection standpoint, is an important variable in choosing the best mortgage. Adam O. Kirwan, J.D., LL.M. dedicates an entire chapter of his outstanding book, *The Asset Protection Guide for Florida Physicians* to this issue. We highly recommend this book for a more in-depth understanding of the *homestead exemption* from an asset protection standpoint. [19]

As mentioned, regardless of the mortgage structures our clients choose, we ultimately want to get every physician into a position where they could, if desired, easily pay off their home by the time they reach their desired financial independence age.[8]

Taking all of the previous factors into account, families with enough assets have at least three strong options to pay off their mortgage:

1. For those families that are not emotionally bothered by mortgage debt, have a low interest rate, and live in a state that does not protect home equity, maintaining a large mortgage balance may be the most attractive option. If you have enough investments to pay off your home, you should be able to structure them to provide enough income to cover the majority of the mortgage payments if needed.
2. For other families who are concerned about their mortgage debt, and have strong asset protection of their home equity provided by state law, paying off the mortgage would likely be the most advisable option.
3. For those doctors who desire to protect their cash flow, but still want to maintain asset protection and tax deductions, they can select a comfortable payment and then maintain only a mortgage balance that correlates to this payment.

Now that we have covered the basics, a couple of other advanced issues come into play as physicians buy larger or multiple homes.

Jumbo Loans

Many doctors and dentists hear the word "jumbo" when they purchase their home. This simply means that the mortgage is greater than $417,000, and as such, it falls outside of the normal lending guidelines.[9] This equates to an increased risk to the lender, which leads to a higher interest rate.

---

[8] This does not mean that we would always suggest they pay off their home at that time, but that they are in a position to be able to do so with ease.
[9] For 2011 for most counties in the U.S.

Recent Example

In one case, to solve this problem, one of our clients took exactly $24,000 out of her investment account to use as a down payment on her home. Why? This kept her mortgage amount under the jumbo limit, thus avoiding the higher jumbo rate on her mortgage. This decision alone should ultimately save this physician tens of thousands of dollars in interest.

Mortgage Deductibility

The mortgage deduction is one of the largest federal tax deductions that most of our doctors still receive in their personal lives. As of early 2012, mortgage deductions are still available for up to $1 million of combined mortgages on your home and one other personal property, for example, a second home at the lake. An additional deduction is also available for interest paid on up to $100,000 of home equity loans for the same properties. Under current tax regulations, this provides for deductions of interest paid on up to $1.1 million of total mortgage loans if they were structured properly. [22]

Recent Example

Jim and Lisa have the following mortgages:

Property	Mortgage Balance	Type	Rate
Primary Home	*$450,000*	*Mortgage*	*4.75%*
Primary Home	*$200,000*	*Home Equity Line*	*6.25%*
Lake Home	*$600,000*	*Mortgage*	*6.50%*
Lake Home	*$200,000*	*Home Equity Line*	*6.75%*
Florida Home	*$250,000*	*Mortgage*	*5.50%*

How can Jim and Lisa optimize their mortgage deductions?

Jim and Lisa should claim 100% of the interest on their lake home mortgage as a deduction. They should also claim the interest on $400,000 of their primary home mortgage. This will take advantage of their full $1 million worth of deductible

*loans. In addition, they should claim the interest paid on
$100,000 of the lake home's equity line of credit (HELOC) to
utilize the additional $100,000 of home equity loan mortgage
deductibility available to them. In both cases, the lake home
mortgage is preferable for deductions as these loans have a
higher interest rate than those on their primary home.*

*Any interest paid on the primary home HELOC, and the
Florida home mortgage, would not be deductible.*

PRACTICAL APPLICATION

The most important aspect of debt reduction is coordinating your debt
reduction strategy with the other important aspects of your financial
life. This way you can put your debt behind you while still ensuring all of
your other goals are being considered at the same time.

Have you examined how your current debt reduction plan impacts your
taxes, asset protection, or retirement planning strategy?

Spend some time prioritizing the following areas, in order of
importance to you at this moment in your life (1 is most important, 8 is
least important):

_____ Funding college for your children

_____ Saving enough for retirement

_____ Purchasing a larger home or vacation property

_____ Buying a business/practice

_____ Reducing debt

_____ Minimizing taxes as much as possible

_____ Keeping access to money for use at any time

_____ Leaving a financial legacy at death

How does debt reduction stack up on this list? Is debt reduction your
number one priority? If so, you might be best served by delaying any
efforts toward meeting your other objectives until your debts have been
eliminated.

If debt reduction is not your top priority, make sure you prioritize your
other more important objectives before making additional efforts at
faster debt reduction.

No area of personal finance is held closer to the vest than debt. Often this is among the easiest areas for which a knowledgeable professional can assist you. Unfortunately, too many people are embarrassed by their debt position. If this is your situation, please do not let pride get in the way of working with someone to find some great solutions. This will benefit you in the long run financially and emotionally.

CHAPTER 3

Risk Management
Protect Your Income

"No one could make a greater mistake than he who did nothing because he could only do a little." – Attributed to Edmund Burke

---

The idea of protecting one's family with insurance is always more relevant when a major need has recently struck close to home. Many of our clients became more passionate about discussing their insurance needs as a result of stories such as these that took place last year:

- In one of our advisor's communities, a local surgical specialist in his late thirties was on vacation with his family, and suffered a life-threatening stroke. Months later, he is still struggling to recover, and his peers have suggested it is doubtful he will ever be able to perform surgery again.

- One of our advisors received an email this year that left him in shock. A potential client, to whom he had been referred a month earlier, emailed him back to say that he had been paralyzed in an accident, and would regrettably not have a need for financial planning services anytime soon.

- A brilliant surgical resident was killed in a freak accident while participating in his favorite hobby. He was in his thirties and left behind a wife and two children.

- A client in his late forties recently learned that his aggressive prostate cancer has now spread into his bones and throughout most of his body. His oncologist has given him four to six months to live.

Each of these incidents has spurred the close friends and colleagues of these physicians to re-evaluate their own insurance plans. Our worst moments as advisors come when our own friends, family members, or clients experience tough times that could have been alleviated with proper planning. It is a sickening feeling to look back and wish that we had pushed someone harder to get his insurance plan in order, even if it was something the client was not excited to discuss.

Very few physicians are excited to talk about insurance. Just about everyone we know would rather discuss investments or planning strategies. To be frank, most doctors we work with–even the multi-millionaires–are still very dependent on their incomes or their assets for financial success. As a result, insurance is a crucial element of a sound financial foundation. The best investment ideas are worthless if there is no money to fund them. To maintain financial stability through life's twists and turns, you must ensure that your income is properly protected.

Several events can damage someone's income:[10]
- A lawsuit (frivolous or not)
- A premature death
- A disabling accident
- A serious medical condition
- A messy divorce

Our experience is that people are rarely motivated to protect against these factors until it becomes relevant in a friend or colleague's situation.

The good news is that it does not take much time or effort to maintain insurance plans, if they are set up right initially. If you are young, healthy, and have a good credit score and driving record, insurance should be very affordable when structured correctly.

The rest of this chapter will focus on the underlying fundamentals of developing a good insurance plan. We will also provide an inside look at how insurance companies and agents operate so that you can become a more informed decision-maker.

One important, but often overlooked aspect of proper risk management is the process of coordinating your employee benefits with the rest of your financial life.

---

[10] List not meant to be all-inclusive.

Employee Benefits–Employee Perspective

Most practices, universities, or hospitals provide some basic insurance and investment options for their employees or owners. The following is a roadmap to understanding important issues as it relates to your group benefits as an employee.

Group Health Insurance

Group health insurance is often more affordable than anything you can purchase on your own, so we suggest most families take advantage of it, if available. The only exception would be a young person (or couple) in great health with no future possibility of pregnancy. In this instance, it might be more cost-effective to use an individual plan or plans rather than health insurance provided by a group. Fortunately, this is one area where being a medical professional usually pays off. Most physicians have access to great group healthcare options.

> **Note:** *See page 202 for additional information about group health insurance for practice leaders.*

Group Long-Term Disability Insurance

What would happen to your family if you took a 100% pay cut tomorrow? Disability insurance provides your family with income in the event that a medical condition or accident causes you to become unable to work. Many employers provide access to a group plan's long-term disability coverage, but these plans are often poorly structured for doctors. The plans have several limitations that need to be addressed to better coordinate your risk protection. Most employers provide disability insurance that protects only 60% of your income, up to a certain cap (caps typically range from $2,500 to $25,000 per month). The benefit you receive if disabled is the lesser of the cap, or 60% of your income. Because physicians traditionally have higher-than-average incomes, many of them are subject to this benefit cap.

A decrease in income to this degree would be a big problem for most doctors and dentists. Additionally, most group disability plans only provide Tier 1 or Tier 2 coverage and do not offer true "own-occupation" coverage for their doctors (see page 45 for further information on why this is a big problem). For this reason, we recommend first acquiring as much individual coverage as you can, which will vary depending on your income and specialty, and stacking your group coverage on top of this other coverage to protect as much of your income as possible.

> **Note:** *See page 43 for further information on individual disability insurance, and page 204 in the Practice Management chapter for best practices on structuring a group disability plan.*

Group Life Insurance

Another benefit offered by most employers is group term life insurance. A small amount is often provided free of charge to employees, with the option to purchase additional insurance. It is always prudent to compare the price of this additional insurance with other coverage available to you individually in the marketplace. If you are young and healthy, it is likely that you can acquire coverage more affordably by purchasing it on your own instead of purchasing it through your group.

401(k), Retirement Plans, and Stock Options

These important employee benefits, retirement plans and other investments are addressed in the Investment Management section beginning on page 56.

Basic Insurance

Along with employee benefits, other insurance coverage needs to be coordinated in most families' financial lives. This includes:

- Auto Insurance
- Homeowner's or Renter's Insurance
- Liability Insurance
- Own-Occupation Disability Insurance
- Long-Term Care Insurance
- Life Insurance

Auto Insurance

Quality is as important as price when dealing with auto insurance. What good is the cheapest company if they give you a big hassle any time you need to use your coverage? The auto insurance industry tends to be very cyclical and regional. A company that has been great at paying claims for the past decade may no longer be in the next decade. Additionally, a company that is great to work with in Texas may be very difficult to work with in North Carolina.

The most overlooked aspect we see in auto insurance is the medical payment portion of the coverage–this is the portion of auto insurance that pays the medical bills for those people injured in your car during an accident. This needs to be properly coordinated with your deductible for health insurance. You might be willing to "self-insure" the gap between the two, but you should at least know if this is what you are doing. Also, doctors often have deductibles that are uneven or too low, and are paying for coverage they would never actually use.

Recent Example

A radiologist had a $500 deductible on his auto insurance. When he had a claim for $1,100, he didn't want to turn it in because he knew his premiums would go up–so he paid the claim out of pocket. This was probably a wise move. Even wiser would have been a larger deductible to begin with, keeping his premiums lower. Because he was self-insuring anyway, he might as well have saved money in the process.

Property Insurance

It is imperative that you maintain property and liability insurance coverage for wherever you reside. These five mistakes are the most common we see for homeowners:
1. Physicians insure the land on which their home is located.
2. Their deductibles are too low.
3. They do not insure the full replacement value of their home's contents.
4. They do not maintain an off-site inventory, photos, or a video of their home's contents.
5. They do not properly insure their basement against water damage.

Multiple clients have lost their homes to a disaster. Fires, earthquakes, tornados, floods, and hurricanes can have incredibly costly consequences if these risks are not addressed before the fact. In the same manner as auto insurance, make sure you explore multiple options for your coverage. Most families receive a meaningful discount when their homeowner/renter and auto insurance are covered by the same company.

Liability Insurance

There are instances when the liability coverage provided by your homeowner/renter and auto insurance could be inadequate. To further protect your family beyond the liability coverage provided through your current insurance, you should also maintain an umbrella liability policy.

An umbrella liability policy coordinates with your homeowner/renter and auto policies to provide liability protection above and beyond the coverage offered by your other policies. For example, the $300,000 of liability coverage often provided on auto insurance is probably not enough coverage if you cause an accident that results in the death of another person. An umbrella liability policy of $3 million or more could sit on top of the $300,000 of auto liability coverage, providing your family with a total of $3.3+ million of total liability protection.[11]

Why is this essential? If you are found to be at fault in a case, and do not have adequate insurance, you could be required to pay for the damages out of your future income.

Medical Malpractice Insurance

We continue to stress that not knowing the right questions to ask when making financial and legal decisions can lead to unintended consequences. This is especially true in the area of malpractice insurance. Not understanding the various options and intricacies of malpractice insurance can cost you time and money–and cause major problems with your medical credentials.

This is how it often works: One doctor asks another, "Which company do you use?" and he purchases that plan without any further investigation into the important issues surrounding the type of coverage provided. This is great for the insurance company, but not always great for the doctor or dentist. The following sections provide the essential knowledge base for choosing medical malpractice insurance.

---

[11] As your net worth or income increases, you can acquire more sizeable amounts of liability coverage. It is not uncommon for physicians to have $5 million or more of this coverage for a current cost of less than $1,000 per year.

Competition Benefits the Physician

When everyone uses the same company, this greatly reduces competition–allowing the company to set rates to their advantage. In fact, in some states, there is very little malpractice insurance competition, so pricing varies greatly from state to state. Understanding competing options by researching them, either on your own or through your financial advisor, can have a significant impact on your rate.

Recent Example

A sole practitioner's medical malpractice insurance was due to be renewed. Before he signed up with them again, he contacted our firm to ask if his rates were reasonable. To answer, we took the following steps:

- *Reviewed his policy provisions and current rates.*
- *Worked with him to figure out his protection goals for his practice, in coordination with his state laws and hospital credentialing requirements.*
- *Found a new insurance company that was well respected, met his objectives, and cut his premiums by 30%.*

What happened next surprised the physician. His original carrier came back with a lower bid, dropping their fee (which they told him one week earlier was NOT negotiable) in half! Bottom line: A little competition cut this doctor's premium in half, saving him more than $10,000 per year.

Different Types of Coverage

Doctors and dentists need to understand the difference between "claims-made" and "occurrence-based" coverage. The best way to explain the difference is through a timeline.

Malpractice Timeline

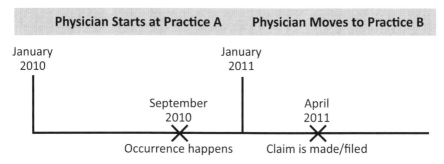

In the timeline above, note that the physician was working with a different practice in 2010, before switching practices at the beginning of 2011. The occurrence happened in September of 2010 while the physician was still at Practice A, but the claim was not made/filed until April of 2011, when the physician had moved to Practice B.

If the physician had occurrence-based coverage while at Practice A, he would still be covered for the event that happened in September 2010, even though he was no longer with that practice. However, if instead the physician only maintained claims-made coverage while at Practice A, he would not be covered for the September 2010 incident. Instead, he would need tail coverage to pick up where his claims-made policy left off in January of 2011. Understanding this difference, and the type of coverage that you hold, is especially important anytime you consider joining a new practice.

Recent Example

A surgeon was changing jobs from one state to another. He was very excited about his new position, but his excitement was quickly quelled when he discovered that he owed $180,000 to his prior practice. He had claims-made coverage–meaning that once he left his former group, he would no longer have coverage for anything that occurred while he was with that practice. In order to protect the practice, his original employment contract required that he buy "tail coverage" if he left the practice at any point. Tail coverage provides ongoing coverage for any work done while employed by the previous practice.

Fortunately we found a better solution that was acceptable to him and his former employer, but this would have been a much less surprising issue had he understood both the contract he originally signed with his employer and the claims-based policy he carried.

Risk/Retention Groups and Captive Insurance Companies

In response to the non-stop increase in malpractice insurance premiums over the past decade, many physicians are now creating risk/retention groups and captive insurance companies in order to better control costs. Through these structures, the member physician "owns" a portion of the entity. Provided that claims are minimal, the profits of the entity are distributed back to the doctors.

Premiums for risk/retention groups or captive insurance companies are usually substantially lower due to the doctor members' ownership. This also gives the potential for a tax break to the physicians, provided that the risk/retention group or captive insurance company is well structured.

Practices with more than ten doctors often pay between $200,000 and $250,000 in annual malpractice premiums for the group. Right now OB/GYN doctors are hit especially hard, often paying $50,000-$100,000 in premium each year *per physician*. In the above example, if ten OB/GYN physicians came together to form a risk/retention group or captive insurance company, they could likely reduce their premiums by half or more.[12]

Questions to Ask

These are questions you ought to know the answers for regarding your malpractice insurance:

- How much coverage do you have, and are the limits commensurate with your state laws?
- When was the last time you shopped for competitive rates?
- Do you know what your coverage actually is–and what its limits are?

---

[12] Risk retention groups and captive insurance companies have several risks associated with them. Consult with qualified legal and insurance professionals prior to implementing either of these strategies.

- Does your coverage have a "hammer clause"–a statement inside the policy that details the insurance company's right to settle a claim? In other words, if you get sued, do you have the right to determine if the case is settled, or does the insurance company maintain this right?

Physicians fail to realize until it is too late that many insurance companies prefer to *settle claims* out of court instead of fighting them. The problem is that a settled claim shows up on your professional record. It is important to make sure that it is your choice whether the case gets settled–and not the insurance company's, especially if you have no fault in the case.

> **Doctors often need a clean record to keep their license or credentials, and most don't know realize this until it is too late.**

Own-Occupation Disability Insurance

As mentioned before, we recently learned a client had been diagnosed with aggressive prostate cancer that has since spread into his bones and other organs. Immediately life was put in perspective for his family. When we met for an update at their home, this client's primary concern was about his disability insurance. He wanted to make sure his family would be okay if he was unable to work for an extended period of time. This client has been the sole breadwinner for his family for a number of years, but they are not yet at a point where they are financially independent without insurance.

We quickly reminded the family that they had well-structured disability insurance in place (three policies working together), and that they would be just fine financially no matter the direction this cancer took. This client had set out a clear mandate years earlier when he told us, "My objective is to take care of my family whether I live too long, die too early, or get disabled along the journey." His courageous outlook, in spite of this traumatic experience, is inspiring–but it also emphasizes the need for every doctor to make sure his or her disability insurance is well thought out.

When it comes to designing your personal disability insurance program, three important issues work together in determining your best outcome:

1. How much *net* income you desire.
2. The strength of the insurance coverage available.
3. How to best coordinate individual insurance benefits with group benefits.

Income Protection Desired—After Taxes

Determining the correct amount of net monthly income you desire is the most important factor when evaluating your disability insurance needs. We highlight *net* because disability benefits are either paid out *income-taxable or income tax-free*, depending respectively on whether 1) you or your practice took a tax deduction for the premiums paid or 2) if the premiums were not deducted.

As previously stated, most physicians receive some basic coverage from the practice, group, university, or hospital with whom they are affiliated. This is often equivalent to a percentage of pay (for example 60%) up to a maximum cap–anywhere from $2,500 to $25,000+ per month, depending on the employer.

Physicians should complement their group disability coverage with individually owned disability insurance coverage. The question becomes, "How much additional coverage is appropriate?" The answer is found in the following formula:

Net Income Desired If Disabled $ _____

SUBTRACT −

Group Benefits Available _____

ADD +

Tax Owed on Group Benefits

_____

$ _____

**Amount of Individual
Coverage Needed to
Properly Protect Your Family**

Strength of Coverage

The proper amount of coverage is important–but equally important is the strength of the coverage. To simplify this issue, we divide policies into three tiers of available coverage.

Tier 1 "Any Occupation" Coverage

Tier 1 coverage is the weakest form of disability insurance. A Tier 1 plan states that if you can work in any profession, you are no longer disabled. Even though you can no longer work as a physician, if you can answer the telephone, you are no longer disabled because you could work as a receptionist at your office. Many group disability insurance policies provided by a university or hospital start as Tier 2 or Tier 3 coverage, and quickly turn into Tier 1 coverage after two years of disability. As faulty as this coverage is, it is much more prevalent than many physicians and practice managers realize.

Recent Example

A specialty surgeon lost a limb due to a freak accident. He was unaware that the $10,000 per month of disability coverage he was receiving from his group plan was scheduled to run out after his second year of disability. His policy was "specialty specific" Tier 3 coverage for the first two years of his disability, and it reverted into Tier 1 coverage thereafter–meaning that he would stop receiving benefits, even though he could no longer practice his surgical specialty.

Tier 2 "Specialty Specific–Not Working" Coverage

Tier 2 coverage is anecdotally the most common for physicians, but we usually cringe when we encounter specialty physicians who own it. Tier 2 coverage pays a benefit if you cannot work in your specialty, provided that you are also not working in any other capacity. In other words, if you cannot perform surgery, but you can still conduct office visits–and want to continue doing so to maintain your partnership status in the practice– you would no longer be considered disabled. The same would be true if you wanted to teach or move into hospital administration.

Tier 3 "Specialty Specific" Coverage

Tier 3 coverage is what the specialized physician should own whenever possible. Tier 3 coverage has a simple definition that says you are disabled if you cannot perform your specialty. Period! If you cannot perform the duties of your specialty, you are disabled, and should receive full benefits. It does not matter if you work elsewhere, teach, conduct office visits, or move into administration. If you can no longer perform your specialty, you are disabled. The good news is that a properly structured Tier 3 plan frequently has the same cost, or often less, than a Tier 2 plan.[23]

The above details lead to the conclusion that it is very important to make sure you understand which Tier your individual and group disability insurance policy falls into in order to ensure that you have not accidentally acquired Tier 2 coverage.

> **Just because you were told that you have "own-occupation" or "specialty-specific" coverage does not necessarily mean that you have a true Tier 3 plan. Not all specialty-specific coverage is created equally.**

One of the biggest problems we encounter is that some insurance agents actually masquerade their Tier 2 coverage as Tier 3 coverage. We have an email on file that was forwarded to us from a physician. His insurance agent, from a popular mutual insurance company, was boldly misleading his client about this issue. He was "assuring" the client that his disability coverage was better than anything else on the market, when it was clearly Tier 2 coverage instead of the stronger Tier 3 coverage.

The worst part was that the agent apparently did not even understand the contract for the coverage he was selling, because he misused several terms and described things inaccurately to his client. We put the physician in direct contact with the underwriters from the insurance companies so that he could ask his specific questions. After doing so, the physician immediately opted for the stronger Tier 3 coverage instead of the weaker Tier 2 coverage. It also happened to be less expensive.

Properly Combining Coverage

One final issue, important to many higher-income specialists, is how to properly combine multiple disability insurance policies. For higher income specialties, three policies are often at play that must work hand-in-hand to be structured as efficiently as possible:

1. Your "base" individually owned policy
2. Your "secondary" individually owned policy
3. Your group policy from your practice/employer

The finer details of how to properly combine these three policies are beyond the scope of this book. However, at a basic level, it is important to know that whenever possible, it is essential to put your individual policies (base and secondary) in place *before* you join your group or take on your group coverage because group coverage counts against you when determining the amount of coverage for which you are eligible. Conversely, individual coverage does not usually count against you when determining the amount of group coverage available.

> *This issue is addressed further in the Group Benefits section beginning in page 191 where we show those in leadership roles how to best structure group coverage for their practices.*

The good news from a cost standpoint is that disability insurance is a temporary solution. Once your assets are sufficient and can provide for your family on their own merit, disability insurance is among the first a physician can afford to reduce or cancel. Think of it this way, when you are young, your debts are high, and your assets are low, so your need for coverage is likely to be the greatest. As you reduce debt and acquire assets, your need for coverage should continue to decrease.

Recent Example

A fifty-year-old physician was worried that he had the wrong definition of disability on his insurance policies. After looking at his big-picture financial plan, we realized that he no longer had a need for disability insurance going forward. He cancelled his disability policy and acquired a long-term care insurance policy instead, still saving money in the process.

Long-Term Care Insurance

Long-term care insurance covers people who need nursing home or home health care for an extended period of time. Many people do not have enough assets to afford this coverage, while others have enough that they can self-insure. The candidate most commonly in need of this coverage is a person in his or her forties or fifties, with assets in the range of $1 million to $3 million. If your assets are valued at over $3 million, and there is no strong history of Alzheimer's disease in your family, you may be in a position where either self-insuring or using a hybrid product may make more sense.[13]

Another case where long-term care insurance may be desirable is when you know you will need to help provide for your parents in retirement. Some physicians acquire long-term care insurance policies for their parents, with the idea that they are prepaying some of the expenses they would pay later anyway. Some states offer a family policy that will provide coverage for up to four people within the same family. The advantage: If the parents do not use it, it will provide protection for the doctor and her spouse later on.

It is important to note that this issue could be addressed very differently, depending on your state of residence and marital status. For example, Indiana and New York currently offer unlimited asset-protection benefits for those who pay for the minimum standard of coverage.[14] Thirty-eight other states provide partial asset protection for consumers if they have long-term care insurance. [24] Additionally, some long-term care insurance companies provide a discount as long as someone is married, but other companies only provide a discount if both spouses acquire coverage. Understanding these nuances can lead to as much as a 30% cost savings when seeking coverage options.

Recent Example

The above concept made a tremendous difference for an oncologist we work with who wanted to provide coverage for

---

[13] A hybrid product is one that provides protection for long-term care, but also pays a death benefit if the long-term care insurance is never utilized. This is sometimes described as "the affluent way to do long-term care insurance."

[14] Indiana and New York are currently the only two states to offer unlimited asset protection from Medicaid asset rules, provided that minimum policy standards are met. [24]

his mother. After our client's father passed away, our client's mother remarried. The client wanted to provide coverage for his mother, but not her new husband. We found a company that would provide her with a marital discount simply because she was married, whereas many of the companies wanted them both to purchase coverage in order to provide a large marital discount.

Note: *See page 205 in the Practice Management section for how some medical groups integrate long-term care insurance into the benefits provided to doctors.*

Life Insurance

The final component of a properly balanced insurance program is life insurance coverage. Few insurance topics are as widely debated as: 1) how much coverage should be owned, 2) and what type should it be?

Life Insurance During Phase I: The Lean Years

During Phase I, the above debates are irrelevant, and the answers are simple. Let's face it, your family has a lot to lose without you, and your income, in the picture. Many young doctors and dentists stand to earn more than $10-$25 million in income over their working years. Imagine suddenly losing that income stream when something like cancer or a car accident takes away that potential for your family. The way to properly protect against this is to acquire meaningful amounts of life insurance protection.

During Phase I of wealth building, we suggest getting as much inexpensive, *convertible,* term-life insurance as possible. Because we work with dozens of companies, it is not uncommon in our process for husband and wife to end up with coverage provided by different companies. Why? Most companies have a niche where they are most competitive. For example, one company is a specialist for people who fly airplanes as a hobby. Another company is great for people who are a bit overweight. Some companies penalize applicants for poor family health history prior to age sixty, but others push this age back to seventy. Only one company that we are aware of currently ignores nicotine gum usage when considering health status. The list goes on, but the bottom line is that considering only one company for your coverage is not likely to provide the best options. By switching companies, some clients have actually been able to triple their life insurance coverage with no increase in cost.

The Right Amount of Coverage

Doctors and Dentists often ask: How do I calculate the right amount of coverage to protect my family? It is actually much simpler than many people realize. Take the amount of income you would like your family to have in the event that something happens to you. Plug this number into the following formula, and you will have a basic guideline for the right amount of coverage to acquire.

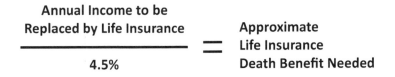

$$\frac{\text{Annual Income to be Replaced by Life Insurance}}{4.5\%} = \text{Approximate Life Insurance Death Benefit Needed}$$

> **Recent Example**
>
> *A client wanted to replace $300,000 of his income for his family in event that he dies prematurely. This amount divided by 4.5% dictates that he should acquire approximately $6,650,000 of coverage to ensure that his income is no longer needed for his family–and that they can adjust their needs for inflation each year.*

In other words, you need $1 million of life insurance coverage for every $40,000 to $45,000 per year of income that you want to offset. Either the $1 million can be used to pay down debt, which should free up the need for $45,000 per year of income, or alternatively, it can be turned into an income stream.

Initially most people are surprised by the large number when they plug their income need into the formula, but keep in mind that at this point in life, your need for coverage is as great as it is ever likely to be.

Fortunately term life insurance is incredibly affordable. If you are healthy, you can acquire meaningful amounts of coverage for a very reasonable cost. For example, $5 million of twenty-year term life insurance coverage on a 35-year-old male with a great health rating costs only about $2,000 per year, as of the date this book was written.[15]

You need $1 million of life insurance coverage for every $40,000–$45,000 per year of income that you want to offset.

That said, we cannot stress enough how important it is to acquire the proper amount of life insurance coverage right now. You will never be younger or healthier than you are today. One small change in your health can cause a drastic increase to your cost of new coverage.

Recent Example

A physician client put off acquiring term insurance coverage because he wanted to complete his residency training first. Unfortunately, he got cancer in his last year of residency. Now, even though it is completely in remission, it will need to stay that way for a minimum of five years before any life insurance company will make him a reasonable offer. Even then, his coverage will be very expensive. His pursuit of saving a few dollars during residency is costing him big, because he did not lock in his young, excellent health when he had the opportunity.

Stay-at-Home Spouses

For spouses who do not work outside of the home, most of our clients typically acquire $500,000 to $2 million of term insurance coverage so that debts could be eliminated or a nanny could be hired.

Additionally, because these policies are often changeable to permanent

---

[15] Assumes the insured is in great health and receives a "preferred-best" health rating.

policies with no further health underwriting, they may also be used to help mitigate the impact of estate taxes down the road or be used to provide a tax-sheltered investment account option.

> **Note:** *More on these topics in the Irrevocable Life Insurance Trust (ILIT) section beginning on page 134, and the Investment Life Insurance section on page 65.*

Life Insurance During Phase II and Phase III

Once a family moves into the Disposable Income Phase (Phase II) of their financial life, they are in a position to begin making some longer-term decisions about life insurance coverage.

Term life insurance is a great solution for Phase I, but it has two potential flaws during Phase II and Phase III.

1. Term insurance is *temporary* in nature, while death is a guaranteed life event that happens 100% of the time.
2. Term insurance does not provide access to the tax shelter that many of our doctors want for their investments. This tax shelter is provided through permanent coverage that is designed to last until the day you die.

For some families, term insurance is the most appropriate during Phase II. If you are in a lower income specialty, have poor health, or have access to an incredible pension plan through your practice, it might be just fine to hold term insurance until your assets have grown to the point where you can drop this coverage, and save the premium dollars.

Though this advice would hold strong for the typical American family, we have found that most affluent physicians could use life insurance to accomplish one or both of the following objectives. In addition to providing temporary protection for their family, *properly structured* permanent life insurance can provide:

- A *guaranteed death benefit* for your entire life that will help to mitigate the estate taxes that may occur.
- An *extremely tax-efficient investment* vehicle by minimizing the cost of insurance in order to supplement the use of other tax-advantaged retirement plans.[16]

---

[16] Under current tax guidelines

The most important issue is to determine up front which of the two above-mentioned objectives you are trying to accomplish. Completely separate insurance policies are typically warranted in order to most efficiently achieve each of these objectives. A common mistake is improperly commingling coverage to try to accomplish both objectives with only one policy. This is rarely a good move.

Tennis players know that there are two places on the court where it is most effective to be–and one where it is not.

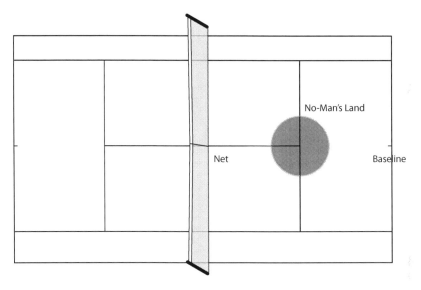

You can either be up at the net swinging away or you can be at the back of the court volleying, but you should rarely be in "no-man's-land" at the middle of the court. This is exactly what people do when they try to commingle their death-benefit needs with their investment objectives. They are putting their life insurance in "no-man's land," where nothing will be efficient. Unfortunately, this is exactly where most life insurance policies we encounter sit, because they were not established properly.

For now, just remember that if you want a death benefit that lasts forever, your objective is to minimize premiums as much as possible in order to achieve this guarantee. This means that you want a policy with as little cash value as possible; hopefully none at all. By getting rid of cash value, you have limited yourself to the minimum outlay required to guarantee a death benefit for life. This structure can sometimes decrease premiums by up to 50%, as compared to a typical whole life policy–a huge cost savings.

Alternatively, if you are looking to use life insurance as a tax-efficient investment to supplement your other retirement accounts, you will want to maximize your investment value. This is frequently a great strategy for young, healthy physicians, and is accomplished by *"over-funding"* a smaller death benefit by as much as possible. This will help to minimize insurance expenses. Ultimately, for those high-income doctors who are young and healthy, the insurance expenses are likely to be far less than the tax cost you would incur if investing in a taxable account instead of a tax-advantaged account.

> ## No one-size-fits-all approach works when it comes to life insurance.

Prior to implementing a life insurance program as part of your financial plan, consider these important facets:

- Only an experienced advisor with an extensive background in this area can make sure that your family has the proper coverage necessary.
- Make sure that your advisor actively works with many insurance companies so that they can find the best possible fit for your unique circumstances.
- Finally, the quality of the company that you put your family's trust in is also important. Rather than relying exclusively on ratings firms that receive compensation from the very companies they rate, we utilize other resources to help determine which companies are right for our clients.

PRACTICAL APPLICATION

To maintain financial stability through life's challenges, you must ensure that your income is properly protected. Not knowing or not understanding what you really have or need could be a mistake you cannot afford to make.

The level of expertise varies greatly from one insurance advisor to the next. The products that different advisors have available also varies widely. Insurance is a commodity, so your goal is to get the best coverage at the best price. Companies often give different advisors different pricing based on the volume of business they produce. Think of it like a bonus for productivity in the medical world. Once a certain quota is met, advisors receive preferred pricing they can offer to their clients. This can lead to discounts as large as 60% on certain products. Therefore, it is essential to work with insurance advisors who gain economies of scale by working with enough physicians to get preferred pricing for you.

Life and Disability Insurance

To properly determine the correct amount for these types of coverages, the most important determinant is how much income you want to replace for your family in event something happens to you.

How much income (after taxes) should be protected for you?
_____ / month

Your spouse?
_____ /month

There is *no* one-size-fits-all approach when it comes to life and disability insurance, and your financial phase of life will be the best determinant as to which type of coverage is most appropriate for your family.

Medical Malpractice Insurance

Answer these questions to uncover the best course of action for your specific needs:

- When was the last time I shopped for competitive rates?
- Am I responsible to pay for tail insurance if I leave my current employer?
- Do I know what my coverage actually is–and what its limits are?
- Does my coverage have a "hammer clause"–a statement inside the policy that details the insurance company's right to settle a claim?

CHAPTER 4

Investment Management
Stop Giving Away Your Growth

"Those who have knowledge don't predict. Those who predict don't have knowledge." – Lao Tzu, 6th Century BC Poet [25]

"The single most important variable in the quest for equity investment success is also the only variable you ultimately control: your own behavior." – Nick Murray, from his book, Simple Wealth, Inevitable Wealth [26]

During a physician's recent investment review with one of our advisors, he began the conversation by asking, "Since the market is so crazy right now, should I continue to keep putting my money into it, or are there better things I should be considering?"

Questions like this have been common over the past several years with as volatile as the market has been. The sad truth is that most doctors today–even the highest-income doctors–are not adequately preparing for the two biggest expenses that are headed their way in the future:

1. Retirement
2. Their children's education

It is not because they do not care about these things. Instead, our experience is that many doctors and dentists simply do not know the most efficient means to plan ahead for these expenses, and volatile markets quickly erode their confidence in whatever attempt at planning they have already made.

> **Compounding the problem is the fact that the average investor actually keeps less than half of the growth that the market has to offer.** [27]

To counter this lack of knowledge, this section provides a framework for investment management. Much is discussed, from the different investment vehicle options to implementing a sound investment philosophy. The issue of investing for your children's education is covered in the following chapter to help ensure that your goals for their education are properly covered as well.

Recent Example

A 56-year-old physician came to our office with his numerous account statements.

He shared in a solemn tone, "This is embarrassing but I have been earning over $500,000 per year for the past two decades, and I feel like I have nothing to show for it. I have put over $2 million dollars into investments throughout my career, and today I only have $1.2 million left. Where did I go wrong?"

Many different types of investment accounts are available. Prior to moving into this discussion, we want to make sure every reader can connect with a few basic terms.

Basic Investment Terminology

Stock: A certificate representing ownership in a corporation. As the corporation grows or earns profits, the investor typically earns a proportionate share of these profits or growth.

Mutual Fund: An investment that pools money from several investors to invest money in multiple investments, such as stocks or bonds. Most mutual funds have a stated objective. Example: "To invest in stocks of foreign companies."

Index Fund: A mutual fund whose portfolio seeks to duplicate a certain basket of stock prices. Example, an S&P 500® Index Fund seeks to duplicate the performance of the 500 stocks tracked by the S&P 500® index.[17]

Institutional Asset Class Fund: A mutual fund whose portfolio seeks to maintain a certain segment of the market at all times. Similar to an index fund, but not tied to the arbitrary basket of stocks within the index. Instead, institutional asset class funds are tied only to the asset class that they represent.

Sub Account: Similar to a mutual fund, but purchased inside of an insurance contract, such as variable life insurance or variable annuities. May be managed by the same manager of a comparable mutual fund and hold similar investments, but is technically not the same thing.

ETF (Exchange Traded Fund): An investment very similar to an index fund except that it trades like a stock. As a result, more options exist for ownership of ETFs than index funds.

Bond: A certificate representing a loan made to a corporation. Typically a set interest rate and length of time are established for the company to repay the loan to the investor.

Benchmark: Most investments can be measured against a particular basket of stocks or bonds. The true test of a stock, bond, mutual fund, or hedge fund is how it performed, compared to its appropriate asset class.

---

[17] S&P 500® is a registered trademark of Standard & Poor's Financial Services LLC.

Investment Accounts

For purposes of simplifying the complex world of investments we have divided the types of investment accounts into these three main categories:

1. Tax-Deferred Accounts
2. Taxable Accounts
3. Tax-Free / Tax-Advantaged Accounts

This terminology may be new to you, so we will explain each account type, and how it works. When it comes to the three account types above, we like to think of them as three different buckets where physicians can put their money. How the bucket functions is determined by how it is treated from a tax standpoint.

Taxation of Investments
How Each Account Type is Taxed

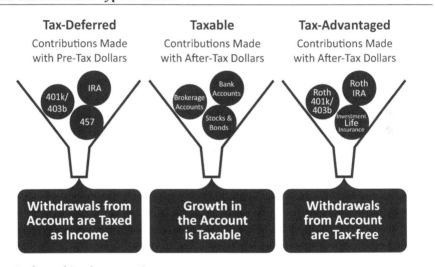

Tax-Deferred Retirement Accounts

Tax-deferred or pre-tax accounts are the most common type of retirement account. In a pre-tax account, you put funds into the account out of your income prior to paying tax on them. The account grows with no taxes being owed until you withdraw your funds in retirement.

Taxation of Tax-Deferred Retirement Accounts

Common Tax-Deferred Accounts:

401k/457
403b/TSA
Profit Sharing
Simple IRA
SEP IRA
Traditional IRA
Pension
Keogh Plan
HR10

The above accounts are funded with pre-tax dollars, and grow tax-free until retirement. Often an employer provides a contribution to accounts such as these on behalf of an employee. For example, if you work at a teaching hospital, they might provide a plan that automatically contributes 10% of your salary, up to a maximum limit, to a 403(b) account for your benefit.

> **Most physicians have never examined the impact that taxes from these pre-tax accounts can have on their financial situation once they are retired.**

Though these accounts are important, they often cause major tax problems down the road. The main problem being that as the account grows, so also does the future tax burden. In other words, while your account is compounding, your tax burden is also compounding. Think of the taxes that you save up front as a loan from the U.S. Treasury. Eventually you pay the initial taxes you skipped, *plus taxes on all of the growth* from your account. This is not necessarily bad, but it is something to be aware of and plan around. Most physicians we encounter initially maximize funding to these accounts, without realizing the tax problems that this can cause in retirement.

Recent Example
A high-income surgeon had established a 401(k) through his practice. He was shocked to learn that he would owe over $1 million dollars in taxes on his pre-tax account throughout retirement.

Another issue to consider when working with pre-tax accounts is that it is very difficult, and sometimes impossible, to access these funds prior to the government-defined withdrawal age, which is currently age 59½. If you take money out of the account prior to this age, you will typically owe a 10% penalty, in addition to your taxes. Under current tax rates, this would equate to a 50%+ hit to the account for most of our clients.

Also, rather than deferring taxes forever, these accounts eventually force you to withdraw funds. The government has established tables that determine the exact minimum amount that must be withdrawn every year beginning at age 70½, and the penalty for not withdrawing funds as required by the government table is currently a 50% penalty tax.[28] Recent research has indicated that the withdrawal rates imposed by the government on these accounts may actually be dangerous to IRA owners, and cause them to run out of money too soon in retirement if they actually spend the funds they are required to withdraw. [29]

Additionally, while these accounts can be very effective at deferring taxes during your lifetime, they are often among the absolute worst places to have money when you die. Estate taxes and income taxes can combine to take away 75% or more of the account in the event of death. This means that only 25% (or less) would actually be available to pass on to your loved ones.

Note: *For further information, please refer to the Estate Planning section beginning on page 123.*

While these accounts can provide substantial wealth for you in retirement, keep in mind that they carry a potentially heavy tax burden down the road, and should not be used as the sole means of providing for your future. However, by properly coordinating pre-tax accounts with tax-free and tax-advantaged accounts, they can actually become a much better tool for retirement.

Tax-Free and Tax-Advantaged Accounts

Tax-free and tax-advantaged accounts are funded with after-tax dollars. The account grows tax-free, and can be used tax-free in retirement, as long as certain guidelines are followed.[18]

Taxation of Tax-Free Retirement Accounts

Common Tax-Free Retirement Accounts:

Roth IRA
Roth 401k
Roth 403b

Life Insurance Accumulated Values

Tax-free accounts, if well designed, are often the savings and investment vehicle of choice for successful physicians. Can you imagine regretting having a tax-free bucket of money available in your retirement years?

The downside of tax-free accounts is that many high-income families are not permitted to use some of them under current law. For example, the right to make contributions to a Roth IRA is not available to any couple that earns over $183,000 per year. [28] As a result, one of our major planning focuses is on designing strategies to help high-income doctors and dentists gain IRS-approved access to these accounts.

One little-known benefit of the tax-free or tax-advantaged accounts is that there is often access to a portion of your funds *prior* to age 59½, if needed, without tax penalties or interest to repay.[28]

---

[18]All accounts considered in this book to be tax-free or tax-advantaged require that specific rules be followed in order to maintain this tax-free or tax-advantaged status. Please consult with a qualified tax accountant to ensure adherence to these rules.

Roth IRAs

The most well-known tax-free account is the Roth IRA. Roth IRAs are funded with after-tax dollars, but the funds inside the account grow and can be utilized tax free as long as the rules are followed. Many physicians believe that they earn too much money, and thus are no longer eligible to make contributions to Roth IRA accounts. While this is true on the surface because of the $183,000[19] income limit , beginning in 2010 a back door was opened by Congress, which currently allows higher-income families to still effectively make Roth IRA contributions.

To do so, instead of funding a Roth IRA directly, a physician can first fund a Traditional IRA, then convert the funds to a Roth IRA. Since January 1, 2010, anyone is permitted to *convert* his or her Traditional IRAs to Roth IRAs *regardless* of his or her income amount.[20] As a result, we now have clients with incomes in excess of $1-3 million per year making Traditional IRA contributions and immediately converting these contributions into their Roth IRA accounts. The beautiful part is that if the Traditional IRA contribution was made with non-deductible (after-tax) dollars, upon conversion, only the gain in the account will be taxable. Our clients typically do their conversions within a few weeks of the contribution so there are generally no taxes owed.

> **Note:** *If you have other Traditional IRA balances, this strategy may not make sense for you due to an IRS limitation that does not allow you to single out non-deductible dollars for conversion, even if you have kept the dollars segregated into separate accounts.[28] This is a common error that we have seen physicians and CPAs alike make, so be sure to pay close attention to this issue if you have Traditional IRA balances that were accumulated from either a rollover or from pre-tax contributions.*

Rule of thumb: if you do not want to convert your *entire* Traditional IRA balance, it is probably best not to make non-deductible contributions and convert them over to your Roth IRA. The good news is that the IRS

---

[19]2012 income limit if married; if single, the 2012 income limit is $125,000.
[20]Prior to 2010, the rules prohibited anyone earning more than $100,000 in AGI from converting a Traditional IRA to a Roth IRA.

aggregation rules do not link spouses, so even if the strategy does not work for you, it might still work for your spouse.

Roth 401(k) & Roth 403(b)

Beginning in January of 2008, Congress allowed for a new type of retirement plan to be established by a *group* for the benefit of its employees. It is a simple twist on the 401(k) or 403(b) plans that are already prevalent. With this twist, plans can add on a *Roth* feature that allows participants to make contributions with after-tax dollars that grow and can be utilized tax-free, similar to its Roth IRA cousin. The two main differences between the Roth 401k/403b and the more traditional Roth IRA are:

1. No income limit prohibits high-income earners from making Roth 401k/403b contributions. In other words, physicians can make contributions to this type of plan regardless of their income.
2. The Roth 401k/403b has a much higher contribution limit of $17,000, as compared to the lower $5,000 limit for Roth IRAs.[21]

Be aware of these two other caveats:

1. We do not always advocate the use of the Roth 401k/403b, even if it is available. This decision needs to be made on a situational basis, as there is no cookie-cutter answer to whether or not you should be using the Roth option.
2. The Roth option still has not been made available by many plans. At the time of this writing, most private practices we encounter have adopted the plan provision, but several universities and hospital systems have not.

Roth IRA Conversions

Even if you are not looking to make new contributions to a Roth IRA as described previously, it still may be prudent to convert your Traditional IRA into a Roth IRA. Doing so, you will pay the taxes on the conversion when you file that year's tax return. Whether or not this idea works in your situation is another question that can be answered only on a case-by-case basis. One important guideline is if you cannot afford to pay the taxes owed on the conversion out of pocket, or out of a taxable account,

---

[21]2012 contribution limit; subject to change based on inflation rates on a yearly basis.

the conversion's benefits are substantially less [30]; conversions would rarely be recommended in this scenario.[22]

Roth 401(k) or Roth 403(b) Conversions

This is the newest planning strategy hitting the financial landscape as of the date this book went to press. Previously, if someone wanted to convert their 401(k) into a Roth IRA, they had to first make a rollover from the 401(k) plan to an IRA. The problem is that many plans do not allow for rollovers to be made while an employee/physician is still working for the group, so many physicians who desired to make conversions to Roth IRAs were not allowed. Fortunately, this complication now has a solution.

Plans that have adopted the Roth 401k/403b provision can now also elect the option to allow conversions inside of the plan from the Traditional 401k/403b to the Roth 401k/403b.[31] This means that a physician with this option in place could now make the Roth conversion even if still working for the same group.[23] Similar to the other discussions though, this is not an automatic recommendation, and it would be specific to the individual participant whether or not it was beneficial to utilize this plan feature.

Investment/Variable Life Insurance

Investment life insurance is an often-misunderstood means of accumulating funds that can be used in a tax-free manner throughout retirement. A common misconception is that the insurance expenses will weigh down the investment returns, but when compared side by side with a taxable account, variable life insurance often becomes an attractive option that could actually save many physicians $500,000 or more in unnecessary, future taxes. That is real money, so we have become increasingly convinced that this is a strategy worth exploring for high-income wage earners who meet three important criteria. They must:

---

[22]If you are under age 59½ and pay the taxes directly out of the account during the conversion process, you will also be charged a 10% early withdrawal penalty on the amount withheld from conversion to pay taxes. This is in addition to any Federal or state tax owed. A withdrawal taken to cover taxes owed as a result of conversion is not considered a "qualified distribution event." A normal exception where this penalty would be tolerated is for a physician completing a conversion upon graduation from training where ½ of the year's income was much smaller; thereby keeping the physician in a much lower tax bracket.

[23] This change was part of the Small Business Jobs Act of 2010. Consult IRS Notice 2010-84 for guidance on implementing this into a plan.

1. Be young, preferably working for at least 7 more years
2. Be healthy
3. Properly coordinate this strategy with other investment accounts to gain maximum benefits

Note that the above criteria just eliminated most of America's population, so it is important to understand that this is not a blanket recommendation. This is a strategy that makes sense for high-income, executives and doctors who are twenty-eight to forty-nine years old.

Think of investment life insurance similarly to any other retirement plan. Conceptually you deposit funds into investment sub-accounts that are similar to mutual funds, allowing you to focus on strategic diversification across the global market. The funds grow tax-deferred, and can be utilized on a tax-free basis through the ability to take withdrawals and low or no cost policy loans.[25] The end result being you could end up in a position to retire 1-3 years earlier than if you had put these funds into a comparable taxable account.[26] If you are young and healthy, the long-term insurance costs associated with an investment life insurance policy could be significantly less than the potential tax expenses associated with a taxable investment option. Not to mention that in many states, investment life insurance is asset protected from creditors, whereas a taxable brokerage account is difficult to protect in *every* state. This is real money from a strategy that too often gets ignored.

We believe the reason people frequently use insurance incorrectly as an investment is because they do not actually treat it as an investment. We are seeking to maximize the cash-on-cash rate of return on the client's full *deposit.* Many physicians often make the mistake of only paying attention to their rate of return on their *cash value*, and this is a very different equation than one that pays attention to the rate of return on the cash deposited. The cash value's rate of return ignores all insurance expenses, while the ROI on the *cash deposited* pays attention to all investment expenses, and properly accounts for them.

---

[25]The no-cost loans are commonly referred to as "wash loans." Each insurance company creates its own policy and contractual terms for how policy loans will operate.
[26]Assumes taxation of life insurance policies remains consistent, and that the long-term average insurance and administration expense ratio is no more than 1.50%.

Note: *Page 49 in the Risk Management section further discusses some of the intricacies of the protection elements of life insurance.*

Remember, if life insurance is being used as an investment vehicle, it is important to minimize the insurance expenses. This is accomplished by designing the policy specifically to function as an investment–and not worrying about it being your end-all death benefit.[27] Finally, it is also imperative that you work with a high-quality company that provides access to a good selection of investment sub-accounts that follow the same overarching investment philosophy you are utilizing for the rest of your retirement funds.[28]

> **The key: If you are using life insurance as an investment, treat it like an investment.**

Taxable Accounts

Taxable accounts, often referred to as non-qualified accounts, joint accounts, or brokerage accounts, are different than retirement accounts because they can be used for anything you want–a lake home, your children's education, early retirement, etc. Most of the tax benefits that retirement accounts offer are lost, but in turn, the account has far less restrictions on how, when, and why the proceeds can be used. These accounts are funded with after-tax dollars. As your investments grow, they may or may not be taxed, depending on what investment is used within the account. When you ultimately withdraw your money, you pay taxes on any growth in the account that has not been previously taxed.

---

[27] Term insurance can be used as a supplement to your investment policies in order to provide the protection benefits needed to fully protect your income or economic value.
[28] Insurance sub-accounts are similar to mutual funds.

Taxation of Taxable Accounts

Common Taxable Accounts:

Joint Accounts
Individual Accounts
Transfer on Death (TOD) Accounts
Tenants by the Entireties Accounts
Employee Stock Option Accounts

TAX
Only on growth that has not already been taxed

TAX or TAX
Depending on investment type held in account

$ TAX

$ $ $

In coordination with other tax-sheltered accounts, it is important to have funds in this type of account. Why? They can be accessed for any reason at any time, with no penalties and often minimized taxes. In other words, this bucket is an excellent resource for short-term accumulation of funds or emergency reserve dollars. Just understand that for long-term dollars, the tax-free bucket is usually a better resource for your after-tax contributions.

Annuities

Annuities are a type of investment that fit into a category of their own. When you use an annuity, you are using an insurance contract that often has an investment component mixed in. There are many factors to consider with annuities, including special tax treatment and expenses. Because their intricacies are beyond the scope of this book, we will suggest three brief points that doctors and dentists should understand:

1. If you are under age forty-five, you should normally consider an annuity only if you are deeply concerned about asset protection issues–and your state offers protection to annuity values. Annuities have costs that exceed other investment alternatives, like institutional asset class funds. As a result, younger physicians should typically avoid these expenses, unless they are trying to protect assets from a future creditor, or are abnormally market averse.

2. If you are nearing retirement age, and want to protect the principal on a portion of your investment accounts, an annuity may be a highly attractive option. Some annuities are designed with a built-in safety net for investors. The concept is that you can still have gains

if the market does well, but you are protected from some forms of downside market risk if the market performs poorly. Think of this as insurance for your portfolio.

Your comfort level with the market will determine if it is worth the extra expense to protect the portfolio. Many of our clients nearing their retirement years have found annuities that include this safety-net feature are a surprisingly affordable option to provide them with peace of mind about their portfolios. To these physicians, the added expense was well worth not having to worry about another market downturn, similar to 2001 or 2008, souring their retirement.

If used appropriately, the added expense of the annuity has the opportunity to be made up through additional returns from your investments. These are returns you never would have had the potential to receive if you had stayed too conservatively invested because you had no "safety-net" in place.

3. If you are already in retirement, annuities can often be a great fit to help provide a stable monthly income stream for your family. In some interest-rate environments, annuities can offer substantially increased monthly income compared to their bond counterparts. [32]

Esteemed as one of the top annuity experts, Professor Moshe Milevsky was once an outspoken critic against annuities, testifying that investors could create their own safety nets with less cost. However, he changed his philosophy as the market continued to evolve, and had the following to say in his acclaimed 2007 article, *"Confessions of a [Variable Annuity] Critic"*:

> *In the last few years... I am seeing an enormous shift in the way [variable annuity] policies are designed... It is now time for me to update my official position on these instruments... it seems the relative value pendulum has swung in the opposite direction. I can no longer claim that you are being overcharged for these guarantees or that you can achieve similar goals at a lower cost. It would be very difficult and expensive to bake a living benefit in your kitchen.* [33]

We will not spend more time on this topic, but note that annuities are often appropriate for a portion of a physician's retirement accounts once they reach a point within 10 years of retirement, or possibly sooner if asset protection is a consideration.

Choosing the Correct Accounts

Once you understand the different types of accounts available–tax-free, tax-deferred, taxable, and annuities–the question becomes: Which types of accounts are most appropriate for your particular situation? Again, no "cookie-cutter" answer exists. The best solution is usually a combination of the above accounts. Only a thorough analysis of the big picture can provide the proportion of each account that should be used for your family's situation. Some items to consider in making this decision:

- What do you anticipate future tax rates to look like? Is this higher or lower than your current rate?
- Do you already have a sizeable balance in any one account type? Would tax diversification be appropriate?
- Are you receiving a match from an employer to use a certain type of account?
- What are your objectives with the funds? Do these objectives occur prior to retirement?
- What type of investments do you plan to purchase?

> **Please do not take this issue lightly. The difference between which account type is used could mean the difference in millions of dollars of taxes over your lifetime. Taxes play a large role in how easily an account can grow and be used in the future.**

Many physicians mistakenly assume that they will be in a lower tax bracket when they retire, and that this will solve their future tax problems. In order to actually be in a lower tax bracket when you retire, realize that two important variables have to work in your favor at the same time:

1. If tax rates stay the same, you have to earn less income to be in a lower tax rate. If all of your money is tied up in the tax-deferred bucket, earning less income is not always possible because any money you take out of this bucket is counted toward your taxable income. Additionally, remember that as a physician, your definition of

"lower income" will still likely place you among the top 5-10% of U.S. wage earners. As a result, it is a mistake to expect that your tax rate will be substantially less in retirement.

Consider this, if you are earning $500,000 today, your federal tax rate is 35%. If you reduce this to $250,000 in retirement, and use the tax-deferred bucket to provide this income, you would still be in the 33% income tax bracket. At 2012 tax rates, your income would have to drop below $142,700 before you would enter the 25% bracket.

We agree your income will probably be lower, but the better question is: Will it be low enough to make a meaningful difference to your future tax bracket?

2. You also have to hope that you retire at a time when Congress is using a low tax rate. Right now, we are at a very low rate of taxation in our country's history. Many physicians forget to factor in what we call Congressional Risk into their thought process about their future tax rate.

To put it bluntly, even if you make less money in retirement, you may not be in a lower tax rate. It will all depend on who is in office during your retirement years, and what decisions they enact on your behalf. Consider the historical income tax rates for the highest income bracket, compared to our tax rates today:

2012 Federal Income Tax Brackets

Single Tax Payers

Income	Marginal Tax Rate
Between $85,651 and $178,650	28%
Between $178,651 and $388,350	33%
Income over $388,351	35%

Married Tax Payers Filing Jointly

Income	Marginal Tax Rate
Between $70,701 and $142,700	25%
Between $142,701 and $217,450	28%
Between $217,451 and $388,350	33%
Income over $388,351	35%

The key here is to have a good balance of these various buckets so that throughout your retirement years, you can make adjustments and withdraw money from any given year's most tax advantaged bucket.

Recent Example

The State of Michigan provides a great example of why this flexibility is so important. Prior to 2011, retirees could withdraw up to $90,240 per year out of their tax-deferred retirement accounts without being subject to Michigan income tax. This meant withdrawing up to $90,240 of income from the tax-deferred bucket would only cause Federal income tax of approximately $9,700 (a 10.7% average tax). Any additional withdrawals would have been subject to a 25% Federal income tax and the normal Michigan income tax.

In this case, it often made economic sense for a Michigan retiree to withdraw up to the $90,240 limit from their tax-deferred bucket, and take any additional withdrawals from the tax-free/tax-advantaged bucket to avoid the much higher taxation. The rules changed in 2011 when Michigan passed an updated budget that allows this Michigan tax-free withdrawal for only those residents age sixty-seven and older. It is now much less attractive to make a withdrawal from the tax-deferred bucket for a physician younger than age sixty-seven. [34]

As you can see, having both the tax-deferred and tax-free buckets available alleviates the chances that a legislative change, such as this, could have a major impact on your retirement taxes owed.

**Having both buckets at your full disposal gives you the permission to determine your own tax rate in any given year during retirement.
That is the position we want for every physician.**

Investment Options

Once you establish which type of investment accounts to use, the next step is deciding which investments to hold in those accounts. Though investment options are virtually unlimited, we have chosen to address the four primary investments we see physicians successfully use:

1. The market
2. Practice ownership
3. Real estate
4. Exotic / private opportunities

The Market

Most physicians use "the market" as their primary vehicle for wealth accumulation. When we say "the market," we are referring to publicly available investments that tend to trade easily. For example, you may have heard of small caps before. This refers to investing in small companies. Large caps are large companies. The market is not limited to only investing directly in companies. Instead, money from one investor can be grouped together with money from another investor to gain access to more investment choices with less cost. This is known as a mutual fund. Many market components can be used to diversify investments. On page 90 we cover the concept of diversification in more detail. However, simply put, diversification means spreading your assets to multiple investments so that risk is reduced without necessarily reducing growth potential. This works because many types of investments are not highly correlated with one another so that when one is going down in value, others may be going up in value.

When using the market, a physician should focus on asset allocation, low expenses, and tax efficiency, rather than on trying to pick the hot stock or mutual fund of the day. The following table shows many of the various segments of the market available for investment, as well as, historical returns of each of these different types of investments.[29]

---

[29]All returns are in U.S. dollars. Data was taken from a reliable source, but we cannot directly attest to its accuracy. The portfolios referenced above are for illustrative purposes only, and are not available for direct investment purposes. Performance above does not make adjustments for expenses associated with the management of an actual portfolio. 80 year data not provided in the chart indicates an asset class that was not tracked during that time frame. [45]

Investment Type	80 Year Results 1931-2010	20 Year Results 1991-2010
Us Large Cap Growth	9.4%	8.5%
US Large Cap Blend	9.9%	9.1%
US Large Cap Value	11.2%	8.2%
US Small Cap Growth	10.2%	8.2%
US Small Cap Blend	13.1%	12.8%
US Small Cap Value	15.4%	15.6%
Int'l Small Cap	-	7.0%
Int'l Small Cap Value	-	9.2%
Int'l Growth	-	4.7%
Int'l	-	5.8%
Int'l Value	-	11.4%
Emerging Markets	-	12.2%
US Real Estate	-	11.5%
Long-term Gov't Bonds	5.5%	8.5%
Long-Term Corp Bonds	5.9%	8.2%
Intermediate Bonds	-	6.4%
One-Month US T-Bills	3.6%	3.5%

Practice Ownership

Many doctors and dentists receive their income through ownership in a practice. From an investment standpoint, many of our clients earn better returns by investing in their practice than they likely could with other investment choices.

> **Note:** *The section on Business/Practice Management (beginning on page 191) delves into specific issues that owners of medical practices need to address.*

For this reason, many practice owners primarily use the market as a means of diversifying and protecting the wealth they have already created in their business. They often invest more conservatively in the market than our non-business owner clients because they are not relying on the market to create wealth. Their business handles this function. Instead, the market simply serves as a means to protect the wealth that their business has already created.

Real Estate

Real estate became a hot investment during the stock market downturn in 2001 and 2002. From 2001 through 2006, many people entered the real estate investment world, only to see their property values decimated between 2007 and 2008. This is not to suggest that real estate is always a bad investment, rather, that successful investors in the real estate market are usually those that treat it as a full-time career. They invest for a living in residential, commercial, and/or developmental real estate, and they earn a good living doing so. The point is that you probably need to choose which one you want to be–a real estate tycoon or a physician– because it would be rare to see someone who is great at both.

Rental property is not often the easy lottery ticket to wealth that infomercials promote it to be. Owning one or two rental properties can quickly turn into a losing proposition. Consider the example of a client who made a profit of only $150 per month after paying for his mortgages on two properties. All it would take is one month without a tenant, or a large repair, for the entire annual profit to be eroded.

We question the logic of investors who get into real estate as a hobby or for the chance to make a quick buck. Why take on the headaches and the risk of leverage in the real estate industry? This return could often be matched with far more conservative investments that do not involve the use of debt. Instead, we advise physicians to avoid direct real estate investments outside of the scope of their normal business unless they want to take on another full-time job. Instead they should consider the market as their primary wealth driver.

The good news is that investors can still gain great exposure to real estate without taking on the risk of debt–or additional work. This can be accomplished through the market by acquiring investments called Real Estate Investment Trusts (REITs). REITs function like mutual funds where investors pool their resources. Commercial property, mortgages, and other real estate investments can be purchased in bulk with a share of the profitability (or losses) returned to the investor, with no additional work or debt required. REITs are considered to be the most efficient way to achieve broad diversification in the real estate industry.[35]

Many physicians believe that this is a great alternative to active involvement in real estate projects outside the scope of their medical practice. We agree philosophically. Unless the individual real estate deal comes as part of the package with your practice ownership, it is probably best to leave it alone.

Exotic / Private Opportunities

Several other distracting opportunities exist for physicians outside of the normal stock market–primarily because most medical specialists qualify as "accredited investors." An accredited investor is one that has a net worth in excess of $1 million (excluding a primary residence) *or* has income in excess of $200,000 to $300,000 per year. The income component alone qualifies most physicians as accredited investors.[30]

Why does this matter? Because accredited investors have access to investment options that are prohibited from being sold to the general public because they are considered to be too risky.

Many physicians are excited by the concept that they have access to investment opportunities that others do not. The relevant question again is: Does it matter? The short answer is that your status as an accredited investor means very little, but your status as a properly credentialed physician could mean much more. To clarify, it will help to understand the various exotic opportunities out there.

Hedge Funds

Unlike mutual funds, hedge funds are able to bet against the market (called "shorting" the market), and they are also allowed to borrow against your money to seek larger returns. Does it work? Consistent studies suggest not. There is no evidence to support that hedge funds perform any better than should be expected from random chance or luck. This is largely

An accredited investor is one that has a net worth in excess of $1 million OR has income in excess of $200,000 to $300,000 per year.

---

[30] $200,000 from a single individual or one earner in the family, or $300,000 if combining both spouses' incomes.

in part due to the high fees charged by hedge fund managers, typically ranging from 4.26% to 6.52% per year.[36]

Private Equity

Private equity deals fare no better, and the risks are much greater. Venture capital, leveraged buyouts, and mezzanine financing deals require substantial risk on the part of the investor. You give up liquidity, diversification, and transparency for the *chance* of a big payoff. What do you stand to gain from this? Studies show the payoff is not worth the risk. The returns gained through private equity dealings are no better than those provided by investing in small cap (company) publicly traded stocks. [36] In other words, historically speaking, you would have gained the same returns with more liquidity, diversification, and transparency.

David Swenson, famous for his outstanding track record managing Yale's endowment fund, had these remarks for individuals considering private equity deals:

Understanding the difficulty of identifying superior hedge fund, venture capital, and leveraged buyout investments, leads to the conclusion that hurdles for casual investors stand insurmountably high. [37]

Exotic investments are not worth the risks they pose. Unfortunately, being an accredited investor is not as advantageous as it sounds.

Recent Example

A client received a phone call from his banker who wanted to tell him about the new private equity deals they had exclusively available to "high-income investors" like him. The banker was promoting an offshore oil drilling expedition that would tie up our physician's funds for eight to ten years. When we analyzed the deal for the doctor, we learned that the expected return was far less than the historical return of small cap (company) stocks. This meant he would take more risk, and have less access to his money, for the opportunity to possibly earn less growth.

Normal exotic investments do not add as much value as hoped, but your credentials as a physician (not your income), might sometimes grant you access to excellent investment opportunities not afforded to the general public. An increasing trend for physicians is to hold ownership interests in surgery centers, ancillary services, and hospital syndications.

Ancillary Services

We find it much more logical for physicians to attempt to outperform the market when they can directly affect the outcome. Ancillary services can generate additional income for you–ultimately meaning that you do not have to rely as much on seeing more patients to maintain a similar income stream.

Many ancillary services may be available, depending on your specialty. The idea behind investing in ancillaries is that because you are referring out the business, you might as well get paid for the additional work to be done. When physicians ask what ancillary services they should consider offering, we ask them what business they are referring out the door the most. That is probably your best place to begin strategizing.

Hospital syndications are also increasing in popularity with healthcare reform underway. Ownership of a hospital gives you access to some of the profits. The requirement that you be a physician who has credentials at the hospital keeps the public from gaining access to the investment opportunity. Hospitals sometimes treat physician ownership as a means of doing profit sharing, whereby you get to participate in the profits of the place you already do the work.

When a physician considers ownership of ancillary services, we ask him or her to address three issues up front:

1. Does the opportunity have a good business model that makes sense, and does the financial data support it?
2. What is the exit strategy for the future in the best-case and worst-case scenarios?
3. Is the return worth the risk?

To clarify the first issue, it is helpful to examine the financial ratios of the service in question in order to get a feel for how those compare to what would generally be expected for a similar business.

Recent Example

A surgeon was considering buying into a local surgery center. Everyone told him it was paying a 20% dividend every year, and that it was a slam-dunk investment. He was wise to ask to see the historical financial records up front. By looking at the historical income statement, balance sheets, and cash-flow statements, we were able to determine that the surgery center's financial health seemed to be deteriorating rapidly.

After some local investigation, the physician found out that the orthopedic group was selling out its ownership in the surgery center, and had been winding down scheduling there. This was a big potential problem because the orthopedic group accounted for more than 40% of the work being done at the surgery center. This meant losing the orthopedic work would take away any profits the new physician could have expected.

The financial ratios are the diagnostic tool that helps you measure whether or not an opportunity makes good business sense. You need to know what the difference between a good ratio and bad ratio is—or hire someone who does.

The exit strategy is something you want to consider anytime you enter into a business relationship.

- How do you plan to sell your shares of the hospital syndication?
- Will the buyer of your medical practice logically also want to acquire the ancillary business you have established?
- What could happen to the value of your ownership if Stark laws are increased, and you can no longer own any portion of an ancillary service?

The best business opportunities are those that offer little risk in terms of how the exit strategy will impact you personally.

Finally, if the above questions have reasonable answers, the last step is to determine whether the potential reward is worth the risk. A general rule is that it is not worth the loss of liquidity on any of these services, unless you expected to earn 15% or more on the investment returns.

A surgery center that returns only 8% in profit each year would not be worth the risk, unless you had reason to believe that your group's involvement would increase surgeries enough to increase the profit margin to the 15% minimum requirement.

In summary, exotic investments available to the general public are rarely a good opportunity, but direct access to additional revenue on work you are already generating can often be very profitable. This might be the best exotic investment it makes sense to pursue. Diversification remains paramount, so we would not want to see more than 15% to 25% of someone's investments tied up in these types of investments. Instead, the open market offers the best long-term opportunities to be properly rewarded for the risks that you take.

The next section will give you a strong primer on the academic, disciplined approach to investing that we believe should guide the long-term growth for the majority of doctors and dentists.

Market Investment Strategy

When it comes to investing in the market, physicians tell us that the three things they desire are:

1. Growth
2. Reduced volatility
3. Asset protection

Investment Growth and Reduced Volatility

As it relates to investment performance and volatility, the typical investor thinks that 2% was a bad year, and 14% was a good year. However, performance is always relative. What if the market benchmark had a loss of -5% in the year that your account earned only 2%? You actually had a great year. What if instead, the market benchmark was earning 20% in the year that you only received 14%? You had a bad year. Performance is king, but it must be accurately gauged, and this is done through a process of properly benchmarking your investment results against market expectations.

The number one contributor to why people fail to achieve wealth through the market: They fail to understand how risk works, and as a result, their emotions get the best of them.[26]

When it comes to increasing investment performance and reducing volatility, we are aware of six items that physicians often believe have an effect on their investment results:

1. Investment selection
2. Market timing
3. Diversification
4. Taxes
5. Expenses
6. Investor behavior and overconfidence

Sound investment strategy seeks to maximize the efficiency of each of these elements in order to provide the best investment returns possible. In the medical world, physicians are constantly looking at the data to determine if there is a better way to do something. Much of this data comes out of research completed at some of the world's most prestigious academic institutions. The financial sector has similar research occurring. Unfortunately, the results of this research usually get ignored because they fly directly in the face of Wall Street.

In fact, consistent studies show that focusing on investment selection and marketing timing produce long-term results far worse than one should expect from random chance or luck, and yet, Wall Street concentrates its mantra on these strategies. As you go through the following section, realize that we believe there is no better approach to investment management than one that is academic and disciplined; rooted in science instead of anecdotal evidence.

Investment Selection

Most physicians will admit that they do not believe someone can consistently pick the hot stock or the hot fund, but when we examine their investment portfolios, this is exactly the strategy most doctors are implementing as their primary investment focus. They do this by selecting mutual funds managed by analysts with this very charge.

Adding to the confusion, some investment managers inevitably beat the market in any given year. The relevant question becomes: Can an investor expect an investment expert to consistently beat the market throughout their working years? We contend studies show this is a losing proposition.

An ongoing study by The Center for Research in Security Prices (CRSP) at the University of Chicago's Booth School of Business, documents the percentage of equity investment managers who fail to perform to the standards of their market benchmarks.[38] If analysts and fund managers are as good as they believe they are, we would expect these percentages to be far greater.[6]

Failure of Equity Funds

Percentage of Active **Equity Funds** that Beat Their Benchmarks
January 1996 - December 2010

	Value	Blend	Growth
Large Cap	37%	16%	21%
Mid Cap	4%	6%	3%
Small Cap	18%	7%	17%

The statistics for bond analysts and managers are even worse.[38]

Failure of Fixed Income Funds

Percentage of Active **Fixed Income Funds** that Beat their Benchmarks
January 1996 - December 2010

	Government	Corporate	Muni	High-Yield
Short	3%	2%	0%	10%
Intermediate	13%	8%	0%	

Note that a few investment managers do outperform their benchmarks over extended periods of time. The relevant question remains whether or not someone could select these managers from the crowd in advance. Further evidence strongly suggests the answer is "no." Eugene Fama

(University of Chicago Booth School of Business) and Kenneth French (Tuck School of Business at Dartmouth) completed a study of mutual fund managers to determine how their results compared to those that should be expected from random chance or luck. The result (see graphic below) was that the managers actually performed worse than what should be expected just based on random chance.[39]

Random Chance vs. Skill

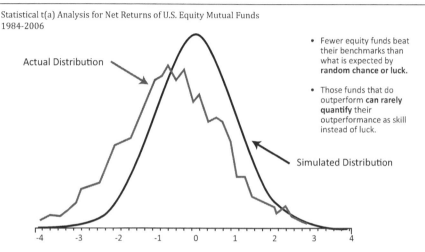

Statistical t(a) Analysis for Net Returns of U.S. Equity Mutual Funds 1984-2006

Actual Distribution

- Fewer equity funds beat their benchmarks than what is expected by **random chance or luck.**

- Those funds that do outperform **can rarely quantify** their outperformance as skill instead of luck.

Simulated Distribution

In other words, even if a manager has outperformed the market in the past, does this mean that he can continue to do so in the future? How can we answer this question when we cannot even identify if the manager's ability to out perform was due to skill, or instead, to being one of the lucky few that we would expect to see?

The anecdotal evidence for this point is overwhelming. Consider the following examples of Morningstar®, Warren Buffett, and Peter Lynch.

Morningstar®

Morningstar provides its Morningstar Rating™ system to provide "a quantitative assessment of a fund's past performance–both return and risk–as measured from one to five stars... As always, [it] is intended for use as the first step in the fund evaluation process". [40] / [31] In other words, Morningstar's goal is to identify investment managers that, based on their formulas, have performed the best historically.

---

[31] Morningstar and the Morningstar Rating are trademarks or service marks owned by Morningstar, Inc.

Let's now examine a sampling of how these star ratings actually translate into future results for investors. The following graphic shows the distribution of Morningstar's star ratings among a 1,615-fund sample set.[32]

Morningstar Ratings

Is There Predictive Power in Morningstar Ratings?

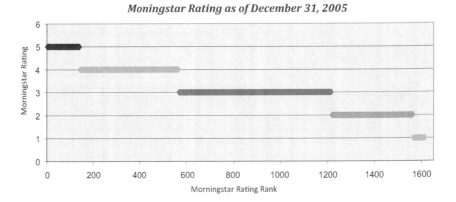

Moningstar Rating as of December 31, 2005

As you can see, less than 200 funds in the sample set received their prestigious 5-star rating, approximately 400 received a 4-star rating, and so forth. Unfortunately, the investor's incorrect expectation is that these star ratings should mean something about the future performance of this mutual fund, believing a 5-star fund should outperform a 1-star fund, and so forth. Consider the following evidence:[33]

[32] For illustrative purposes only. Sources: Mutual fund universe statistical data money managers' fund data provided by Morningstar, Inc. Sample size (1,615 funds) take from entire domestic equity universe with an inception date prior to January 1, 2001. Past performance is no guarantee of future results.

[33] For illustrative purposes only. Sources: Mutual fund universe statistical data money managers' fund data provided by Morningstar, Inc. Sample size (1,615 funds) taken from entire domestic equity universe with an inception date prior to January 1, 2001. Subsequent 5-year period represents existing funds from the Morningstar Rating as of December 2005. Past performance is no guarantee of future results.

Morningstar Results

Subsequent Five-Year Performance of Morningstar Rated Funds

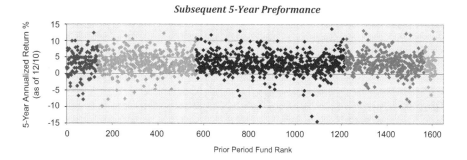

Subsequent 5-Year Preformance

The Morningstar Rating™ system had no apparent bearing on the actual future performance of the underlying mutual funds. What you are seeing, and we believe will continue to see, is that investment managers, economists, and analysts are great at being able to describe what just happened. However, not surprisingly, they are awful at being able to predict the unknown future.[6]

Warren Buffett

So, if Morningstar fails to pick the hot future performers, how about the "Oracle of Omaha," Warren Buffett? Statistically speaking, there is no doubt about it: Buffett's long-term results do outperform the market. The relevant question again is if there is anything you as an investor can gain from this now? The latest research shows probably not. In his recent paper titled *Deconstructing Berkshire Hathaway* [41], Weston Wellington analyzes Buffett's performance over the past twenty-five years, as compared to the benchmarks deemed the most relevant.[34]

---

[34] The 25-year benchmark is the S&P 500® index. Due to Berkshire Hathaway's movement toward a more global portfolio, the 15- and 10-year benchmark referenced is the Dimensional Equity Balanced Index.

Warren Buffet

The Oracle of Omaha vs. the Benchmarks *(Average Annual Returns from 1986 to 2010)*

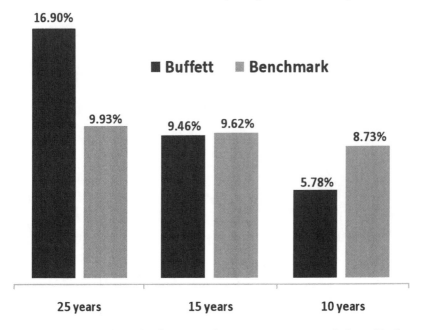

As you can see, if you had invested your money in Berkshire Hathaway twenty-five years ago, you would have handsomely outperformed the market. The story is quite different though, if you began investing ten years ago. You would have actually underperformed the benchmark by almost 3% on a year-by-year basis. Why? One theory is the concept of diminishing returns. This theory suggests that those few investment managers, like Buffett, who truly are skilled, attract larger and larger dollars, which require them to find more and more opportunities. Eventually, even those skilled managers attract too much money to keep up with the influx of capital.

Peter Lynch

Peter Lynch also provides a great anecdotal example of this theory. He is another shining example, among few, whose investment results can be statistically attributable to skill rather than luck. [42] From 1977-1990, he guided the Fidelity® Magellan®[35] fund to consistent benchmark-beating performance.

---

[35] Fidelity and Magellan are both Registered trademarks of Fidelity Investments.

What about Mr. Lynch's successors? How has the fund performed since Mr. Lynch's departure? Fidelity Magellan has beaten the S&P 500® index only 8 of the last 20 years since Mr. Lynch resigned.[36]

This is perhaps why Mr. Buffett summed up our sentiments well when he said in an Annual Report to Berkshire Hathaway holders:

> *Most investors, both institutional and individual, will find that the best way to own common stocks is through an index fund that charges minimal fees.[(43)]*

To paraphrase, the best way to own the market is simply to buy the entire market. Even though the data warns so strongly against it, many physicians continue to attempt to pick the hot stock or the hot fund, or they work with advisors who claim to be able to do so. The reality is, almost all of them do little more than look into a rear-view mirror when picking investments. They find mutual funds or individual stocks that have performed well historically, and look at how well their portfolio would have done if they had been in those funds for the past ten years.

However, in most cases, these hot performers end up dragging behind their market benchmarks in the future. It is like being stuck in traffic–the lane next to you always seems to be moving faster. Once you finally switch lanes, that one slows way down, and the lane you were already in gets moving again.

Hopefully we have made a strong case: Trying to pick the hot stocks or the hot funds is not the best way to add value to your investment portfolio. Unless you are holding index funds or institutional asset class funds inside of your portfolio, this is exactly the strategy that most of your managers are trying to implement as the primary means of getting you on track for retirement. We are often concerned by how many physicians are putting most of their eggs in this basket, without even knowing they are doing so.

---

[36] Internal research conducted by Larson Financial Group, LLC, comparing the results of the S&P 500 Index to Fidelity Magellan. Research completed with data provided by Standard & Poors and Fidelity.

Market Timing / Forecasting

Physicians are also engaging in the practice of trying to time the market. This often happens without their knowledge because the underlying fund managers inside of their retirement accounts are engaging in this strategy on their behalf. They do this by moving your money in and out of the market in hopes of trying to catch the wave or avoid the decline.

Recent Examples

We recently analyzed a client's portfolio only to find that he had one fund with 25% sitting in cash, instead of in the market where it belonged. The fund manager is obviously trying to time the market with the client's cash, and the client had no idea that this was going on with his money until we pointed it out.

Another physician pulled his entire portfolio out of the market because the political party he did not like was elected as a majority in his state.

The question again is: Does it actually work to try to time when to get in or out of the market? The answer is that you have to have pinpoint accuracy on the specific days you get in and out of the market in order to add any value from a timing standpoint. Consider the following:[37]

---

[37] Performance data for January 1970-August 2008 provided by CRSP; performance data for September 2008-December 2009 provided by Bloomberg. The S&P data are provided by Standard and Poors Index Services Group. US bonds and bills data provided by Stocks, Bonds, Bills and Inflation Yearbook, Ibbotson Associations, Chicago (annually updated work by Roger G. Ibbotson and Rex A. Sinquefield). Indexes are not available for direct investment. Their performance does not reflect the expenses associated with the management of an actual portfolio.

Market Timing

Performance of the S&P 500 Index from 1970 - 2010
Hypothetical growth of $1,000

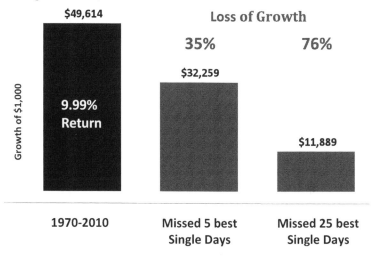

Had you only missed the twenty-five best days of the market in this forty-one year period, it would have cost you 76% of your account value. No joke, missing less than one day per year can have enormous impact on your results. The problem is that you have to be perpetually right when you try to time the market. Right about when to get in, and right about when to get out, and right about when to get back in, and right about when to get back out–perpetually! This is not investing. This is gambling.

Many physicians do not realize that their portfolio is built around trying to time the market. This happens when the fund they utilize lacks integrity, or when they succumb to other fad strategies making their way through the investment world.

A fund lacks integrity in our eyes when it promotes itself as one type of fund, but actually trades like another. For example, a fund may call itself a U.S. Large Cap (company) fund, but instead, it purchases International Small Cap (company) stocks in an effort to beat the U.S. Large Cap (company) market. The occurrence of purchasing stocks outside the scope of a fund's normal objectives is all too common among funds that purport to have beaten their benchmarks. Fortunately, this is easy to analyze with the right tools in place.

A new fad moving through financial firms is using a strategy called "tactical asset allocation." The idea is that the advisor selects the segment of the market that his believes is the next hot place to be, and over-weights your portfolio to that segment of the market. By calling it "tactical asset allocation," it disguises the fact that this is nothing more than a market-timing strategy packaged up with a nice new marketing bow. Choosing the asset class to over-weight "tactically" is trying to time the market by guessing that a certain asset class will soon outperform another.

Rather than trying to guess which way the wind is going to blow, we advocate that physicians should focus their attention on a long-term investment approach. While trying to pick the hot stock at the right time sounds exhilarating, the reality is that few investors will ever do this consistently year in and year out over their investment lifetimes.

So, if trying to pick the hot stocks and trying to time the market are not the correct ways to add value to your portfolio, what are the things that really do matter? We believe properly diversifying, lowering investment expenses, minimizing taxes, and managing emotion are the keys to a successful investment outcome.

Proper Diversification

Proper diversification means spreading your investments around to lots of different baskets instead of keeping them all in one basket. Think of it as a Ferris wheel at the amusement park with many different buckets. If all of your money is in one bucket, and it tips upside down, you will lose everything in it. If your money is in seven to twenty different buckets, and one bucket tips, you should still be just fine. It is rare in the investment world to have most buckets tipping at the same time.

Studies consistently conclude that how you establish your diversification mix is among the most important fundamentals to investing in the stock market. This is why we believe every client should establish a diversification (or asset allocation) policy for their portfolio, and make sure that their investments follow a consistent, holistic philosophy.

Contrary to this approach, most investors do not follow a coordinated asset allocation policy across all of their accounts. Often physicians invest their 401(k)s completely differently than their taxable or tax-free accounts. There is no consistent philosophy and no real rhyme or reason to how each of their accounts is allocated. As investment managers, one of our most important jobs is to make sure that families take a truly holistic approach that coordinates *all* of their investment accounts to a unified purpose that follows a disciplined diversification strategy.

Recent Example

Physicians at the University of Florida have three different retirement plans available: the ORP plan, a 403(b) plan, and a 457 plan. Each plan has a different list of investment options. When U of F physicians are asked why they chose a certain investment mix, they rarely have a methodology. Rather, they picked whatever their departmental colleagues had also chosen. If someone were paying attention to a holistic diversification plan, the doctor would have a clear-cut answer on which plan(s) to choose, which vendors to pick within those plans, and which mutual funds to select from each vendor. The "big picture" should follow a uniform approach, though the individual parts may look completely different from one another.

Why is diversification so important? Consider the results of a Nobel Prize-winning study that identified diversification policy as the root cause of 91% of a portfolio's outcome:[44]

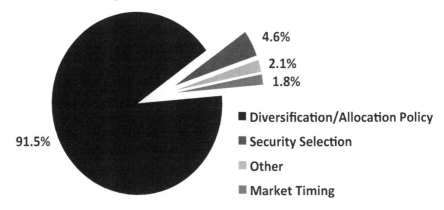

4.6%
2.1%
1.8%

■ Diversification/Allocation Policy
■ Security Selection
▨ Other
■ Market Timing

91.5%

Most physicians admit that their portfolio should be diversified, but when we pull the skin back, we find that most are not properly diversified. This happens for four main reasons--because they:

1. Do not know what they actually have in their portfolio. Take for example the surgeon who believed he had a well-diversified portfolio because he owned four different mutual funds. The problem he was not aware of was that all four of the mutual funds were buying the same stocks.

2. Are taking on the wrong level of risk in their portfolio. They have never synced it properly with their objectives for retirement. In other words, if you do not have to, why take on more risk in your portfolio?

3. Are much less diversified than they realize because they are missing out on a major segment of the market. This happens primarily when investors own index funds or ETFs because they are only designed to track with a small segment of the market. As a result, the portfolio is not as well diversified as it could be. This is part of the reason why our preference is to utilize institutional asset class funds when possible–as opposed to index funds or ETFs–because they are designed to track the entire asset class, and not just a sampling of investment options within that asset class.

4. Also are not diversified across the globe the way we believe they ought to consider. The global market has changed drastically over the past two decades. The U.S. stock market now represents only approximately 40% of the world's equity market.[45] Most physicians we encounter have more than 80% of their portfolio tied up in the U.S. market. We believe it makes sense to diversify globally, just as much as it makes sense to diversify across different domestic asset classes. As a result, we prefer to match our clients' portfolios up with the broader landscape of the global market. This means we do not try to pick the hot country or sector to have client money in, but instead distribute it into the various global markets, based on their overall market weighting.

A proper diversification/asset allocation policy is what allows you to smooth out a long-term investment portfolio. Because you are purchasing different investments that are not directly correlated, when one is doing poorly, another one may not be. This has been shown to actually enhance performance rather than hinder it. This is a big key in helping to manage emotion, which we cover later in this section.

The following table shows the performance of "the market" as discussed by the media, compared to diversified portfolios consisting of several different market segments or asset classes. The results clearly show that risk can be minimized by not putting all of your eggs in one basket.[38]

Historical Averages Discussed by Popular News Media

Individual Asset Class	10 Year Results 2001-2010	20 Year Results 2001-2010
U.S. Large Cap Blend	1.4%	9.1%

Historical Averages of Diversified Portfolios

Individual Asset Class	10 Year Results 2001-2010	20 Year Results 2001-2010
Risk Averse Diversified Portfolio	5.4%	6.9%
Conservative Diversified Portfolio	6.7%	8.4%
Moderate Diversified Portfolio	7.7%	9.7%
Aggressive Diversified Portfolio	8.2%	10.8%
All Equity Diversified Portfolio	8.4%	11.7%

Take a moment to note the ten-year results of the diversified portfolios. Many news journalists have sensationalized the concept of the "lost decade" when describing the market results over the past 10 years. [46] [47] This may be true if looking at only one segment of the market (like U.S. large company stocks), but it's absolutely false when examining a well-diversified portfolio. This is why we find it so essential to properly manage risk within your portfolio.

---

[38] All returns are in U.S. dollars. Data was taken from a reliable source, but we cannot directly attest to its accuracy. The portfolios referenced above are for illustrative purposes only, and are not available for direct investment purposes. Performance above does not make adjustments for expenses associated with the management of an actual portfolio. [45]

Investment Expenses

Many physicians have no idea how much they are spending to own their investments each year. In addition to explicit costs, such as management fees or trading costs, most investors never see the many hidden costs.

Hidden expenses, such as mutual fund transaction costs, 12B-1 fees, and sales loads, rarely show up on your account statement. Instead, they create a drag on your performance. For example, if an account earned 10%, the statement might show only 8%. The investment expenses were 2%, and you, as the investor, never knew about it.

One of the fundamental keys to investing in the market is to make sure that your investment expenses are minimized. It is normal for us to talk with physicians who have over 3% in investment expenses every year that they never knew about. An investment with these expenses would have to earn 13%, just to pay you 10%. Can you see how much harder it would be to get ahead with costs this high?

A recent analysis showed that the average U.S. mutual fund charges an internal (*hidden*) expense of 1.46%, and the average international mutual fund charges an internal expense of 1.64%.[39] On top of this, advisors charge management fees.

> **Keeping investment expenses reasonably low is an important part of increasing investment returns.**

Investment Taxes

Taxes on investments can erode your returns by 40% or more if you are not careful.[40] On pages 59-72 we covered how various investments are taxed differently, and that often a large difference shows up between investment tax rates and income tax rates. The following chart further clarifies how investments are taxed: [41/(48)]

---

[39] Data provided by Morningstar as of April 9, 2010.
[40] Comparing a tax-free account with an account taxed on the growth at ordinary income rates.
[41] Municipal bonds are not taxed at the Federal level but may be taxed at the state level, depending on the bonds purchased and the state in which you live. Some municipal bonds can also cause AMT tax at the Federal level due to their status as private activity bonds. Consult with your tax accountant for specifics in your situation.

Investment Type	How it is Taxed
Bond Income	Usually taxed at normal income rates
Municipal Bond Income	Usually not taxed at the Federal level
Dividend Income	Taxed at investment rates if "qualified"
Bank Interest	Taxed at normal income rates
Long-term Gain on Stock	Taxed at investment rates
Short-term Gain on Stock	Taxed at normal income rates
International Dividends	Often taxed at normal income rates
Growth in Annuity	Taxed at normal income rates

Account Type	How it is Taxed
401(k)	Taxed at normal income rates
Traditional IRA	Taxed at normal income rates
403(b) / TSA	Taxed at normal income rates
SEP/ Simple IRA	Taxed at normal income rates
457 Plan	Taxed at normal income rates
Pension Plan	Taxed at normal income rates
Roth IRA	Not taxed
Roth 401(k)	Not taxed
Roth 403(b)	Not taxed
Taxable Account	Taxed depending on investment type
Growth in NQ Annuity	Taxed at normal income rates
Growth in Life Insurance	Taxed depending on how withdrawn

Take for example an investor who holds company stock inside a 401(k) plan and in a multi-purpose account. While the investment type is the same (company stock), because the account type is different, the taxes owed at the time of withdrawal may be very different.

Remember: The account type trumps the investment type in determining how the income or growth inside the account will be taxed.

- 95 -

We often see investors make the mistake of not holding the right investment type in the right account type. Without proper training, this can be fairly complicated, but it must be taken into consideration when building a portfolio, or you could end up paying substantially more in taxes than is necessary. This is the reality far too frequently. While seeking growth as the primary objective of your portfolio, you are better off holding your bonds in tax-deferred accounts and equities in your tax-free or taxable accounts.[35] Overlooking this issue could cost you twice as much in taxes on an investment gain, simply because the investment was held in the wrong account type.

Investor Emotion and Overconfidence

Although this aspect of the market is often ignored, we believe, and studies verify, that the investor's own emotion, behavior, and overconfidence often creates a larger negative impact on investment returns than all of the other issues discussed above. An annual study completed by DALBAR shows the typical investor, as compared to the S&P 500® index. Though the actual numbers change, the differential between the two numbers remains comparable from year to year.[27]

> **The typical investor perennially underperforms the S&P 500® index, giving up more than half of the returns that the market has to offer.**

This happens largely in part because investors make irrational decisions.

	1984 - 2000	1986 - 2005	1991 - 2010
S&P 500 Index Results	**16.3%**	**11.9%**	**9.1%**
Average Stock Market Mutual Fund Investor	**5.3%**	**3.9%**	**3.8%**
Percentage of Return Lost by the Avg. Investor	**67.4%**	**67.2%**	**58.2%**

In Jason Zweig's book, *Your Money and Your Brain*, he provides evidence for how the human brain works, as related to one's investment life. His findings are spot on with the anecdotal evidence we encounter day in and day out.

When you confront risk, your reflexive brain, led by the amygdala, functions much like a gas pedal, revving up your emotions. Fortunately, your reflective brain, with the prefrontal cortex in charge, can act like a brake pedal, slowing you down until you are calm enough to make a more objective decision. [(49)]

Most strong investment principles are often counterintuitive. Adhering to a disciplined philosophy focused on proper diversification is not intuitive, but it is essential to long-term investment success. Many investors' decisions are driven primarily by greed and fear. Consider how investors reacted at times when the market was volatile:[42]

The Penalty of Emotion

Fear and Greed Lead to Poor Decision Making in the Market

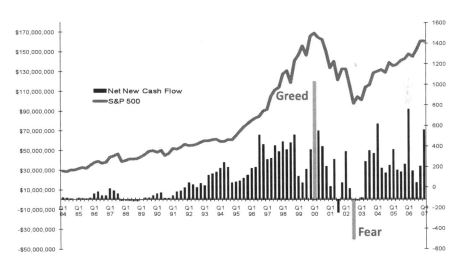

When the market was climbing, investors began contributing a lot more money into the market. When the market was declining, investors pulled their money out of the market. This is the *wrong* way to invest. Investors should be doing the opposite of this, but they allow the amygdala to

---

[42] Data presented by Professor Burton Malkiel, Chair of the Department of Economics at Princeton University at the 2006 CFA Institute's Efficient Market and Behavioral Finance Conference. Professor Malkiel is also the author of *A Random Walk Down Wall Street.*

take over. Instead, they need to slow down their decision making long enough to allow the prefrontal cortex to catch up, and help them to make a logical decision.

Physicians' overconfidence in their own investment abilities picks up where investors' normal emotions leave off. Studies continue to show that physicians are among the worst offenders of having an "illusion of knowledge." In other words, they believe they are more accurate in their investment predictions than they really are. Research analyst, James Montier, suggests, "Doctors are a terrifying bunch of people. When they were 90% sure they were correct, they were actually right less than 15% of the time!"[6] Further studies consistently document that the most overconfident investors are in reality among the absolute worst performers.[5] In *The Investment Answer*, Goldie and Murray suggest that, "We need to understand that overconfidence with regard to investing can be detrimental to our financial health. Success in one walk of life does not automatically translate to success in investing."[50] We share this to confirm that your colleagues are probably not a good source for investment tips, even if they want you to think they are.

Though it is difficult to quantify at the individual client level, protecting our doctors and dentists from their own (and their colleagues') emotional responses and overconfidence, is paramount. It is among a financial advisor's most important value proposition anytime he is entrusted to manage a client's investment dollars. In addition to holistically coordinating all of their accounts, managing for tax efficiency, and keeping expenses low, we also help our physicians maintain a steady course. This alone should pay for an advisor's management fees five to eight times over, if with proper guidance, investors are simply able to overcome their natural tendencies.

PRACTICAL APPLICATION

You would find it foolish for patients to attempt surgery on themselves. Yet, this is what physicians attempt in their own investment lives every day. Overconfidence and emotion are the drivers that cause most investors to keep less than half of the growth that the market has to offer.

Following is a list of questions that can help to demonstrate competency in investment management. Whoever is managing your portfolio should be able to answer these correctly (answers follow):

- Do you purchase individual stocks?
- Do you pay attention to Morningstar Ratings®?
- Do you choose mutual funds based on past performance?
- Are the majority of your investments going to pre-tax plans?
- Are you using index funds or ETFs as your first choice for investments?
- Do you ever make changes to your accounts based on an emotional response to the market?
- Do you look at peer group performance when determining which funds to invest in?
- Are you trying to time when to get in and out of the market?
- Do you get frustrated or nervous after two consecutive negative quarters in the market?
- Do you frequently change investments around in your portfolio?
- Do you pay attention to the mainstream financial media?

- Do you understand the important implications IRS Notice 2010-84 may have on your retirement plans?
- Can you quickly locate your time-weighted rate of return over the past five years?
- Do you have access to institutional asset class funds?
- Do you understand where your risk profile falls in Fama and French's Three Factor Model?
- Are you confident that your risk level is most appropriate for your goals and objectives for retirement?
- Do you have a specific approach determined for how to integrate commodities and inflation-protected bonds into your portfolio?

- Do you have consistent exposure in each asset class in which you invest? (your answer is "no" if you are using index funds or ETFs as your primary investment tool)
- Do you have a plan for international diversification of your portfolio for equities, real estate, and fixed income?
- Are you monitoring your account regularly for rebalancing purposes? Do you do it monthly if you are making ongoing contributions to your portfolio?
- Are you holding the correct asset classes in the correct accounts to minimize your long-term tax burden?
- Do you have a process for determining the risk level of any bonds that you hold? (normal ratings don't count because they are often inaccurate)
- Do you know the expense ratios of the investments you hold? (both explicit and hidden)

Anything above the line should be answered with a definitive "no," and anything below the line should have a definitive "yes." The reality is that we have yet to meet many physicians who can demonstrate a proper handle on these issues. Why are so many physicians so confident in their ability to properly manage their own investments when the list above covers only basic foundational principles? This crisis of overconfidence can cost physicians hundreds of thousands to millions of dollars of lost wealth over their lifetimes.

To be very frank, unless you could answer 100% of the above questions correctly, you are *not* qualified to manage your own investments. The above list does not even fully cover the basics you should understand if you want to manage your portfolio. If you love the rush of buying stocks, set aside an "adrenaline fund" with some play money, and let it ride. However, you cannot afford to gamble with your serious money.

We understand that an overarching problem in our industry is that most financial advisors cannot answer these questions properly either. That is why we give you a list of great questions to ask of any advisor you would consider hiring, beginning on page 212. A true professional will help address these issues and many more for your family. Any fees you pay to them should be more than made up for by properly paying attention to these issues.

> When it comes to investments, an advisor's job is not to beat the market for you. Rather, the advisor's job is to help manage your family's risk within the market and to gain economies of scale that you cannot get on your own.

Your investment policy statement should become the road map that makes sure each of these issues is being properly addressed for your family. It establishes expectations that keep everyone on the same page. Once turbulent times come your way, it also becomes an anchor that allows you to get away from the emotional response your amygdala is pulling you toward. Instead, your unemotionally attached advisor will guide you back to your road map, as that is where your investment decisions should be made.

For further reading:

- *The Investment Answer,* by Goldie and Murray
- *Your Money and Your Brain,* by Jason Zweig
- *A Random Walk Down Wall Street: The Time-Tested Strategy for Successful Investing,* by Burton Malkiel
- *The Calculus of Retirement Income: Financial Models for Pension Annuities and Life Insurance,* by Moshe Milevsky
- *The Little Book of Common Sense Investing,* by John Bogle
- *The Quest for Alpha,* by Larry Swedroe

CHAPTER 5

Education Planning
Avoid the Normal Errors Parents Make

"Economists report that a college education adds many thousands of dollars to a man's lifetime income—which he then spends sending his son to college." –Bill Vaughan, Kansas City Star columnist [51]

Through a recent analysis, a physician learned that it would cost over $500,000 per child to provide the education he desired. This is on top of the private school tuition they pay for their children's elementary and high school education. This story is not uncommon. Education planning is a hot topic for many doctors and dentists. If your income or net worth is, or will be, too high, your family will not likely qualify for any need-based financial aid from the government or a university. The resulting question becomes, "How should we fund our children's education?"

How Much Should Be Funded?
The first step is to define how much funding you would like to provide. The appropriate amount is different for every child, based on his or her capabilities, and your family's values as a parent.

Doctors and dentists often use one of the following four approaches to help determine how much they should set aside for education purposes:
1. Percentage-of-expenses
2. Set-dollar-amount
3. Set savings
4. Cash flow

Percentage-of-Expenses Approach

When we are discussing education funding, the percentage-of-expenses method is the most common approach. Here you determine what percentage of tuition, room, board, and books you would like to fund for your child, and for what type of university. The difference between public and private tuition can be staggering, and you need to plan accordingly.

Set-Dollar-Amount Approach

Through the set-dollar-amount method, a family determines a certain dollar amount that they would like to provide for their children's educational needs. This approach is sometimes more appropriate for a family's situation than the percentage method. Why? Because it controls costs for families that would be financially stretched to provide a large percentage of education expenses for their children.

For example, through this method, a family might establish a goal of providing $150,000 per child for education. If college expenses are greater than this amount, the child is responsible for paying the difference. And, if total cost is less than that amount, some families give the child the excess upon graduating, or allow it to be used for grad school.

The Set-Savings Approach

The set-savings approach has a client designate a certain amount he or she will fund toward education expenses out of discretionary income each month or year. This money goes into an account for education, and whatever accumulates is the assistance provided by the parents.

Recent Example

One physicians sets aside $550 per month per child for education expenses. As his cash flow permits, he increases or decreases this amount. Though he will not know exactly how much will be available when his children go to school, this method ensures they will each have some assistance for education costs without spreading the rest of the physician's financial life too thin.

Cash Flow Approach

Some physicians choose not to set aside funds into an account for education, but rather to pay directly out of their income when their child incurrs these expenses. This approach does not give them the benefit of the tax-advantaged savings options but can still be effective. Families that typically use this method are those with exceptionally high incomes, or those who are already funding private high school tuition out of cash flow.

This approach will likely become more and more difficult to implement due to the alarming increase of tuition at both public and private universities.

Where to Save for College

After you have determined how much funding you would like to provide for your children, the next step is to decide where to save these funds. The five main accounts utilized for education savings include:

1. 529 Education Savings Account
2. Prepaid Tuition Plans
3. Uniform transfers to minors accounts (UTMAs)
4. Taxable accounts in a parent's name
5. Investment life insurance owned by a parent

529 Accounts

529 plans are often our favorite solution for a portion of most families' college savings. Why? 529 plans offer great tax advantages. Many states provide tax savings for funds contributed to a 529 account. The funds grow completely tax-free, and can be withdrawn tax-free for education expenses including tuition, room and board, books, etc.[52]

Taxation of 529 Accounts

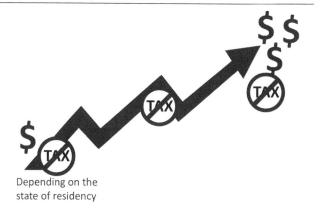

Depending on the
state of residency

Even better than the tax benefits described above, you remain in control of the account forever. In other words, even though your children may be the beneficiaries of your 529 plans, they have no rights or control over the money.

The amount that can be contributed to a 529 account on behalf of a child is potentially limited each year by gift taxes as further described in the Estate Planning section, beginning on page 135. In general, you and your spouse can contribute up to $26,000 total per child per year without running into any tax problems. In addition, the 529 plan has a special tax feature that provides for a five-year acceleration of this $26,000 gift limit.[43] Therefore, you and your spouse can set aside up to $130,000 per child, and completely avoid gift taxes or using up any of your lifetime exemption.[53]

Many doctors and dentists have financially successful parents or other relatives. It is not uncommon for grandparents to set aside up to $130,000 per child for education when they are born. Doing so accomplishes the following for the grandparents:

- It gets the funds partially out of the grandparent's estate, and therefore helps to minimize their estate taxes due.[44]
- The grandparents still completely control the account, and can take it back anytime they want.[52]

---

[43] 2012 gift limit and 529 acceleration limit; subject to change on an annual basis based on previous year's inflation; $26,000 is the limit for a married couple and $13,000 is the limit for a single individual to gift.

[44] Although five years of gifts can be accelerated up front, only $26,000 per year (married couple) is removed from the estate calculation, so it takes five years for a $130,000 contribution to be fully removed from the estate.

- 529s can offer a measure of asset protection and often keep the funds safe in event of a lawsuit.[19]

Although 529 accounts offer numerous benefits, an important downside must be mentioned. If the funds are not used for higher education, the account owner will owe *income taxes plus an additional 10% penalty* on any growth in the account when the funds are withdrawn. To avoid these consequences, the account can be transferred to any other beneficiary in the same family to be used for education purposes. Alternatively, if your child receives a scholarship, penalty-free but still taxable funds can be withdrawn equal to the amount of the scholarship.[52]

A common misconception with a 529 plan is that if a plan is set up in one state, then the funds cannot be used in another state. This is actually not the case. Instead, a 529 plan established in any state can be used for tuition in any other state.

This means that when determining which state's plan to use, you have three main factors to consider:

1. Does your home state's plan offer tax incentives at the state tax level?
2. Which plans have the investment choices that best line up with your overall investment philosophy?
3. If your home state's plan does not have investment options that are the most desirable, then the tax benefits need to be balanced with this issue.

Physicians who have already established 529 accounts are rarely using a plan that we consider a strong choice for education funding. This is perhaps because 529s plans pose a large conflict of interest in the investment world. The plans that we consider to be the strongest are not eligible to be offered through investment brokers. As a result, many investment brokers send their clients to plans that have higher expenses and weaker performance in order to earn a commission from the plan. To put it bluntly, if you purchased your 529 plan through an investment broker, then it is probably not one we would recommend unless it helps you accomplish state tax planning objectives.

Instead, we would suggest working with an advisor who charges an unbiased management fee to help you select the most appropriate no-load, 529 plan for your situation.

Prepaid Tuition Plans

Prepaid tuition plans are a cousin to the 529 plan, and are provided on a state-by-state basis. Conceptually, you buy tuition credits at today's price that can be used later when your children go to college. Although the state-specific plans are beyond the scope of this book, we would suggest in general that some states offer very generous plans, and other states offer little incentive to use their plan. In other words, this is an issue that can only be addressed on a case-by-case basis.

UTMAs

Although Uniform Transfers to Minors Accounts (UTMA) are a reasonable estate-planning tool, we would caution using them for education funding purposes. Through a UTMA account, you simply gift funds to your child. You remain in control of the funds as a "custodian" of the account until your child reaches age 18 or 21 (depending on your state of residence). At that time, the child has full control over the funds, and can use them for whatever purpose he or she desires. Additionally, there are no special tax incentives related to education.

For the reasons outlined above, there are usually better ways to save for education expenses. UTMAs are further discussed as a valid planning strategy in the Estate Planning section as a potential means to avoid estate taxes, or could be a fine tool if your intent is simply to gift money to your children, regardless of how it is used.

Taxable Accounts and Investment Life Insurance

On pages 67 and 65, we discussed taxable accounts and investment life insurance. These investment accounts can be used for any purpose. Many physicians supplement the use of 529 plans by additional savings in a taxable account or investment life insurance. The advantage: You can retain the funds in the taxable account or investment life insurance for your own enjoyment if they are not needed for your child's education.

Recent Example
A physician and his wife are getting serious about education funding for their children, and plan to fund $50,000 per year for education purposes, but do not want these funds to go to a 529 plan. Our analysis found that the best option for this family

was a taxable account, due to the ages of the children. If they had been younger, the investment life insurance would have been another viable option.

Entitlement Concerns

The college experience has become as well known for the parties as for higher learning. As a result, many doctors and dentists want to ensure that their children do not waste their education funds. The family scholarship concept described below is a good option anytime a parent is concerned that his or her child might mismanage resources during college.

The Family Scholarship

Through the family scholarship strategy, parents or grandparents are very upfront with their children about what is expected in order for the child to earn their "college scholarship."

Recent Example

Matt and Wendy have built up over $200,000 in a 529 account for their son, Sam. They have increasing concerns that Sam may not take his education seriously, especially if he does not contribute toward it financially.

Their solution was to establish a "Family Scholarship" for the 529 funds. When he entered his freshman year of high school, they talked with Sam about earning this scholarship. They used the following criteria for their scholarship because they knew Sam could easily meet it if he applied himself in high school. Sam had to:

- *Maintain a 3.0 high school GPA.*
- *Remain free from drug and alcohol use.*
- *Participate in at least one extra-curricular activity each semester.*

The family scholarship idea is not right for every family, but for those concerned that their children or grandchildren might have "entitlement" issues, it can sometimes be a great motivational tool.

How to Invest for College

Once you have determined how much education to fund, and which accounts you plan to use to fund it, the remaining question is: How should I invest my money? Conventional wisdom today suggests that using an "age-based" fund or approach is the best way to go. We submit again that the conventional wisdom may be wrong. As part of our firm-wide research efforts, we are concluding a ground-breaking study. It suggests that age-based portfolios may lead to less opportunity to meet your goals for your children's education. Perhaps it would be better to simply use a conservative portfolio during the entire funding and accumulation period prior to your child going to college.

Why is this? Our theory was simple. You might not have enough time to recover in event of bumps in the market. Whereas you have decades to recover if your retirement account hits a bumpy stretch, education funds are typically exhausted within a few years once distributions begin. Because you have no time for recovery, you have less chance to be rewarded for the risk taken.

As a result, we suggest that physicians analyze their education portfolio risk separately from their retirement portfolio risk. You should establish a separate investment policy in accordance with whatever portfolio gives you the best opportunity to achieve your education funding goals.

PRACTICAL APPLICATION

Education planning needs to be well balanced with providing for your own financial independence needs. Loans, grants, and scholarships are not available for retirement, so most physicians should make sure they have a solid retirement plan in place before venturing into the world of education planning.

Once you do, you must first decide how you plan to fund education (see the several approaches outlined in this chapter). After that, which account types to use can be determined. Do not assume that a 529 plan is always best. The most appropriate course of action depends on your unique circumstances. Sometimes prepaid tuition plans, UTMA accounts, taxable accounts, life insurance, or special trust arrangements can better suit your needs.

Note that your education diversification plan should likely be treated independent from your retirement diversification plan because you are dealing with different time horizons. You have little time to recover from a market slump in education funds, so an age-based portfolio may not be the best use of your money.

Finally, when it comes to 529 plans, many states offer different tax incentives for participation in the home state's plan. Make sure that you properly understand the benefits offered by your state prior to investing in any particular plan, especially because 529s frequently represent a major conflict of interest in the investment world.

For further reading:
* *Savingforcollege.com's Family Guide to College Savings,* by Joseph Hurley

CHAPTER 6

Tax Planning
Stop Giving the IRS 60% of Your Income

---

*"Anyone may arrange his affairs so that his taxes shall be as low
as possible; he is not bound to choose that pattern which best pays
the treasury. There is not even a patriotic duty to increase one's
taxes. Over and over again the Courts have said that there is nothing
sinister in so arranging affairs as to keep taxes as low as possible.
Everyone does it, rich and poor alike and all do right, for nobody owes
any public duty to pay more than the law demands."*
Billings Learned Hand (1872-1961),
U.S. Court of Appeals Judge[54]

A doctor walked into a meeting with his CPA to go over his tax return. He
had billed over $2.5 million for the prior year. "I just don't understand
where it all goes!" he exclaimed.

Of the $2.5 million he had billed, only $1.8 million had actually
been collected. Then midway through the year, Medicare changed his
reimbursement rate on one of his major procedures. As a result, his
collections had taken another $150,000 hit. Then he had overhead of
$720,000. Out of his $930,000 remaining, he had taxes to pay: social
security, Medicare, capital gains, federal taxes, sales taxes, alternative
minimum taxes, real estate taxes, local taxes, and more. When it was all
said and done, his CPA concluded the doctor paid or owed more than
$550,000 in taxes for the year.

Tax Basics

Tax planning is all about using legitimate and legal methods in order to pay as little in taxes as possible. We are not just talking about federal income taxes either, as most physicians pay many other taxes (as noted in the case above):

- Federal income taxes
- State income taxes
- Alternative minimum taxes
- Local income taxes
- Property taxes
- Sales taxes
- Capital gains taxes
- Social security taxes
- Medicare taxes
- Excise taxes
- Motor vehicle taxes

The list goes on and on. The Tax Foundation establishes an annual Tax Freedom Day® and determines each year how long most Americans work just to pay their taxes. In recent years, Tax Freedom Day® did not occur until the end of April, meaning that most Americans spent the first one-third of their year working just to pay their taxes. Our internal calculations suggest that many doctors–without proper planning–will not reach their Tax Freedom Day® until the end of June or later.[45] / [(55)]

It is our moral obligation to pay our fair share of the country's tax burden, but as Judge Hand delivered, our "fair share" is never more than we are legally obligated to pay. The main tax that people pay is Federal income tax. These taxes get proportionately higher as your income increases. Unfortunately, that means that physicians are often among the hardest hit as they have substantially higher incomes than a majority of the population. This chapter focuses on how to stop paying so much money to the IRS – both today and in the future.

---

[45] Tax Freedom Day® is a registered trademark of The Tax Foundation.

2012 Federal Income Tax Brackets

Single Tax Payers

Income	Marginal Tax Rate
Between $85,651 and $178,650	28%
Between $178,651 and $388,350	33%
Income over $388,351	35%

Married Tax Payers Filing Jointly

Income	Marginal Tax Rate
Between $70,701 and $142,700	25%
Between $142,701 and $217,450	28%
Between $217,451 and $388,350	33%
Income over $388,351	35%

As we move into tax strategy, keep in mind that the primary focus is on reducing Federal income taxes owed. A good accountant or CPA will certainly address more than this with you. In fact, a good tax professional can be worth her weight in gold. Unfortunately, many accountants practice what we call "autopsy accounting," where they meet with you *after* the year is already over, and at that time, dissect your tax situation. With that late timing, little to nothing can be done to help you for last year. Instead, a proactive tax professional will meet with you throughout the year, or prior to yearend, to make sure that you are taking advantage of the planning opportunities available.

> The most important thing to look for when selecting an accountant is one that practices proactive accounting, instead of "autopsy accounting".

When selecting a CPA, find one that is familiar with tax strategy. Our experience is that many tax professionals are trained only on how to properly fill out the forms—not on how to help you implement strategies that reduce your tax burden.

Many physicians use our in-house tax firm, MedTax, to handle their tax filing because our accountants are cross-trained in the other aspects of our physicians' financial lives. They are not just number crunchers but instead they understand the strategies that work for short-term and long-term tax reduction.

www.MedTax.com

Tax Strategy
Proactive accountants use tax strategy to reduce your tax burden in three primary ways:
1. Reduce your taxable income
2. Reduce your actual taxes owed
3. Delay the due date on your taxes for many years to come

Reducing Taxable Income
Tax deductions are the means of reducing taxable income as much as possible. Most tax payers are familiar with the idea of deducting the interest they pay on their mortgage from their taxable income. The effect is that there is less income to be taxed. The same holds true for practice owners who are able to expense their business purchases prior to calculating their taxable yearly profit.

The number of opportunities tax payers miss when it comes to tax deductions is astounding. Physicians overpay their taxes consistently by not taking full advantage of the tax deductions available.

Common Tax Deductions Include:
- The value of items or funds given to charity.[56]
- Any interest paid on a first mortgage for your home, and a second home for up to $1 million of loans (see page 31 for further mortgage information). [22]
- Interest paid on second mortgages or home equity loans for your home, and a second home for up to $100,000 of loans.[22]

- Interest paid on student loans if your income is within allowable limits.[52]
- Funds contributed to a tax-deferred retirement plan (see page 59 for information on tax-deferred plans).[28]
- Professional fees that exceed 2% of your adjusted gross income, including legal, accounting, investment, and financial planning fees.[57]
- Investment losses.[48]
- Travel expenses in connection with a job search.[57]
- Expenses for using your automobile for charitable purposes.[56]
- Continuing education expenses.[52]
- Medical expenses, including health insurance premiums, which may or may not have income limits, depending on how the plan is structured.[58]
- Pre-school or childcare expenses paid for your children so that both spouses can work. [59]

Note: *The list is much more extensive for practice owners, but the additional deductions available are beyond the scope of this book.*

Charitable Gifts

Even though numerous tax strategies exist, a favorite tax strategy is applicable to anyone that gives cash to charity each year, and also has a significant taxable investment account. In this case, a physician can gift investments to a charity instead of cash. They can repurchase similar investments with their cash, and will owe less tax when the investment is ultimately sold. This strategy creates a triple tax benefit:

1. You receive a deduction for the full amount of the investments that you gift to the charity.
2. The charity can sell the investments tax-free, even if there is a substantial gain.
3. You pay less tax when you ultimately withdraw your cash that has been reinvested.

Recent Example

Out of their $500,000 income, Scott and Heather gift approximately $40,000 per year to their church. Currently they make these gifts in cash. They also have a taxable (non-qualified) investment account valued at $300,000; $70,000 of this account is gain from two investments that performed very well.

What is the most tax-advantaged way for Scott and Heather to make their gifts to charity? This couple could consider gifting some of those investments that have performed very well. If they want to, they can use their cash to repurchase the exact same investments in their account, but they will have a much higher cost basis now (meaning that they will pay less taxes in the future when the investment is sold again). Their church can sell the investments, even with a large gain, completely tax-free. Everyone wins...except the IRS.

Reducing Taxes Owed

In addition to tax deductions, available tax credits can actually reduce your tax bill, dollar for dollar.

Tax Deduction vs. Tax Credits

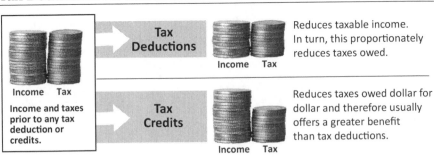

Items potentially eligible for tax credits include expenses for:
- Higher education
- International or domestic adoptions
- Energy-efficient home improvements
- Each child that you have
- Childcare so that you and your spouse can work

Though tax credits are the most desirable tax benefit, they are often excluded for families with high incomes. Therefore, most of our clients find that they are limited only to tax deductions for planning purposes because their incomes are too high to be eligible for any credits.

Recent Example

A client is adopting a child from overseas. The physician and her husband wondered if they qualified for the Adoption Tax Credit because their income is over the $182,520 limit where the credit begins to be reduced. The client determined the best way to get her income under the limit was to defer income into her 401(k) and profit-sharing plans, and work with her practice manager to delay income until the following year. As a result, she should qualify for the full tax credit, and get a refund from the IRS for an additional $13,360 off of her tax bill for the year.[46]

Delaying the Due Date

When tax deductions or credits are not available, a third tax planning strategy is to delay the due date on taxes owed for as long as possible. One respected CPA told us that from day one, a CPA is taught how to keep delaying or deferring taxes. Though this is sometimes appropriate, in many instances it would likely be better to reduce the taxes owed rather than just delay them. Additionally, with high-income professionals, they may actually be delaying their taxes to an even-higher bracket later on. (See numbered list on pages 70-71.)

The problem with delaying taxes is that it usually comes with a cost. Few people understand the negative ramifications of delaying taxes. Take for example the 401(k) that delays taxes until later. Not only do you eventually owe the taxes, but you also owe taxes on the growth in your account.

---

[46] Example based on 2011 tax law. Adoption tax credit legislation is in a state of flux currently and is scheduled to change on a year-by-year basis for the near future.

> **Compound interest has been called the 8th Wonder of the World. Compound taxes are a major problem for retirement.**

Due to the compound taxation often caused from tax-delay strategies, it is usually better to first seek out true tax-deduction strategies. The main exception to this rule comes with major real estate investment. If someone has a large gain on an investment property, under certain guidelines they can do what is known as a 1031 exchange, delaying the taxes owed on the sale of the property by purchasing another property. Many physicians use this technique on their investment property to delay their taxes as long as possible. Provided that they delay the taxes until death, the taxes may be forgiven without ever having been paid.

Alternative Minimum Tax

Surprisingly, many of our doctors find themselves ensnared by the Alternative Minimum Tax (AMT). AMT was established in 1969 after a report was published showing that 155 high-income families paid no taxes in 1967 because they had too many deductions and credits under the normal system at the time.[60]

Over the past three decades, AMT has gone from affecting only 155 families to affecting more than 4 million taxpayers every year. The problem: When the AMT system was established in 1970, no provisions were included for inflation. Because of this error, the AMT tax burden hits more and more families every year, and Congress has not yet fixed the problem.[61]

What is AMT?

AMT is actually a completely separate tax system. In simplistic terms, your tax burden is calculated under two completely different methods, and you owe the higher of the two outcomes.

The families that are the hardest hit are those with incomes between $150,000 and $500,000 that have many children or live in states with high state and/or local taxes. Families above or below this income threshold typically find they do not have AMT exposure under our current system of marginal tax brackets. However, if they fall into the "sweet spot" of AMT, families can expect to owe approximately 27% of their income in Federal taxes. This is not a marginal bracket, but more comparable to a flat-tax system. Compare this to the 22% average tax rate that a family earning $200,000 per year could owe. This is the difference in over $10,000 per year in additional taxes owed on the same income.

Fortunately, some strategies are available that can help reduce your AMT exposure through pro-active tax planning. A knowledgeable accountant is crucial when it comes to this issue.

Uncommon Tax Strategies

Rather than writing an entire book about tax strategy, we have narrowed down a list of six uncommon strategies that could have a big impact on many physicians' tax lives.[47]

The Stockmaster Shuffle

This strategy is named after our good friends Dr. and Mrs. Stockmaster. Dr. Stockmaster is a specialist who utilized one of the greatest contract tax-planning strategies we have seen to date. His wife is a CPA, so between the two of them, they have always been on the leading edge of legal tax ideas. When Dr. Stockmaster joined his first practice out of residency, it occurred to him that he could do much better tax planning if he had 1099 income, but he also understood that he would pay twice as much in social security taxes on the first $110,100 of income because he would be treated as a self-employed individual by the IRS.[48]

To circumvent this problem, Dr. Stockmaster negotiated a split in his compensation between 1099 and W2 income. He received the first $110,000 per year of income as W2 wages, and anything above that his employer paid as a 1099 consultation fee. By doing this, he was able to transfer the burden of the employer side of social security taxes (6.2%) back to his employer. He was still able to do tax planning with the remainder of his income because he was paid as a 1099 consultant. The direct tax savings of this strategy was in excess of $6,500 per year.[49]

---

[47] This book cannot give you personal tax advice, as it would be impossible to do so accurately, without knowing the big picture of your financial situation. As a result, consult with your tax professional prior to implementing any strategy you read about within these pages.

[48] 2012 amount

[49] Note that specific requirements must be met between employer and employee to establish a 1099 relationship. Thanks to Dr. Stockmaster for allowing us to share his idea publicly. Note that the social security tax rate was reduced in 2011 and may be reduced again in 2012, depending on the congressional outcome.

Social Security Refund

Physicians commonly overpay their social security taxes when coming out of training or when changing jobs. This is because social security taxes are due on only the first $110,100 of income each year. When a doctor or dentist changes jobs midyear, they have often paid social security taxes to the treasury through their previous employer. When they go to the new employer, the new employer does not take these payments into account. The physician ends up double paying taxes. Unfortunately, many physicians miss this issue and do not claim their refund appropriately.

Net Unrealized Appreciation

Net unrealized appreciation (NUA) is a great 401(k) strategy applicable to physicians working for a publicly traded company. Typically when a physician purchases investments in a 401(k) plan, any gains are taxed at ordinary income rates rather than at more favorable capital gains rates (see page 95 for a refresher on this). As a little-known caveat in the tax code NUA allows company employees to sell company stock held in their retirement accounts at capital gains rates, rather than at ordinary income rates. Several requirements must be met for this strategy to work, but it can present a great opportunity for physicians working for publicly traded employers. [62]

S-Corp Election or Equipment Rental

If you are a private practice physician, electing S-Corporation status or choosing to rent equipment from yourself, may be a way to avoid paying unnecessary social security and Medicare taxes. The basic idea is that you are seeking to convert "wages" that are taxed by both social security and Medicare to different forms of income that are no longer taxed by either. By choosing an S-Corp election, you might be able to convert income from wages to distributions. Distributions are not taxed by social security or Medicare.

In the same manner, if you utilize equipment that you own in your practice, it may be prudent to rent this equipment from yourself. Though you will still owe income taxes, rental income is also not taxed by social security or Medicare.

Both of these strategies might save you as much as 15% per year in taxes on income converted from wages to distributions or rental income. Again, there are several nuances to be aware of, including state sales tax issues with rental equipment, so be sure to consult with a tax professional prior to implementing either of these strategies.

Fellowship Year Out-of-State Deduction

A final little-known deduction is sometimes available for graduating residents moving out of state from their residency program in order to complete a one-year fellowship. Provided certain strict guidelines are met, it may be possible to deduct your rent, groceries, travel expenses, and several other items during your fellowship year (representing two years worth of tax returns). [63]

Converting Accounts Recievable to Capital Gains if Selling Your Practice

The migration from private practices to hospital ownership is happening throughout the medical world as we write. Often overlooked in the buyout is the ability to convert accounts receivable from income tax to capital gains tax treatment. For high income physicians this could reduce taxes owed on the accounts receivable by as much as 20%. There are several ways to structure this changeover.[50]

A Final Word on Taxes

As your income increases, the number of deductions and credits you are eligible for decreases–and therefore causes you to owe more taxes. At a point, these taxes can become confiscatory, and can force a family to drastically alter their lifestyle. A worthwhile tax accountant will work in conjunction with your financial advisor and attorney to help reduce your tax burden as much as possible.

PRACTICAL APPLICATION

Tax planning is all about using legitimate and legal methods in order to pay as little in taxes as possible. Federal income tax, the main tax most people pay, climbs proportionately higher as your income increases. Physicians are often among the hardest hit by taxes as they have substantially higher incomes than the rest of the population.

---

[50]Special thanks to Art Jensen of the Warner Companies for introducing us to many of these accounts receivable strategies.

Your Tax Strategy

As your income increases, the number of deductions and credits you are eligible for decreases–and therefore you owe more taxes. A knowledgeable accountant will work in conjunction with your financial advisor and attorney to help reduce your tax burden as much as possible.

When selecting an accountant, seek one that practices proactive accounting, instead of "autopsy accounting". Our experience is that many tax professionals are trained only on how to properly fill out the forms–not on how to help you implement strategies that reduce your tax burden.

Many physicians use our in-house tax firm, MedTax, to handle their tax filing because they are cross-trained in the other aspects of our physicians' financial lives, and understand tax strategies. MedTax may be a great option if you are currently only receiving autopsy reports from your current accountant.

Tax strategies can save you money, but what works varies on a case-by-case basis. Remember that deferring your taxes until later is not always the best move.

For further reading:

- *Loop-Holes of the Rich: How the Rich Legally Make More Money and Pay Less Taxes*, by Diane Kennedy, C.P.A.
- *How to Use Limited Liability Companies & Limited Partnerships*, by Garret Sutton, Esq.
- *Individual Income Taxes*, by Willis, et al.

CHAPTER 7

Estate Planning
Create a Legacy and Disinherit the IRS

---

*"He is no fool who gives what he cannot keep
to gain that which he cannot lose."*
– Jim Elliot, Christian martyr [64]

In a recent meeting, a surgeon's wife made a statement that rings true for many physicians, "We've been meaning to get our wills updated for months, but we're always too busy. Now he's busy for the next four months because everyone has met their insurance deductibles, and wants to get their procedures done fast. Please make sure we stay on it and get it done early next year. What is it again that we need to fix?"

Stories like this are all too common. You are busy, and it's easy to push aside the future to deal with the present. We are talking about your children's well being though. We encourage you to review your progress in estate planning in light of the information contained in this chapter regardless of your current financial phase. You could be self-sabotaging the meaningful legacy you could be leaving to others. Even worse, you could inadvertently be naming the IRS as your primary beneficiary. We will get to those topics, but first we will start with the basics.

When we talk about estate planning, we are simply discussing the idea of deciding for yourself, ahead of time, what you want to happen in event that an untimely death, disability, or health emergency should occur. This chapter will address three key areas as they relate to estate planning:

1. The Basics

    How to get started, what pitfalls to watch out for, and what tools are available to help your family.

2. Financial Implications
   The death/estate tax, and how it impacts planning for many
   physicians.
3. Advanced Issues
   Other issues you need to be aware of, especially as it relates to
   multi-generational planning issues, non-U.S. citizen spouses, and
   community-property states.

The most important part of building a sound estate plan is to first clearly
define your family values. An estate plan should be values-based, or it
will never accomplish your goals. In fact, estate planning experts Cochell
and Zeeb ardently claim:

> *Nine out of ten inheritance plans will fail, destroying the very families
> that they were designed to protect.* [65]

Values-Based Estate Planning Basics

Values-based estate planning is all about deciding ahead of time to whom
you want to leave your assets, and for what purposes. You have a choice
among the following beneficiaries:

- Your loved ones
- Your favorite charities
- A nursing home
- A thief
- Your spouse's next spouse
- The government

Which of the above do you prefer? The only way to ensure that your
wealth goes to the loved ones and/or charities of your choice is to take
the proper planning steps ahead of time.

People often find it difficult to discuss these issues, and as a result,
they do nothing. What they fail to realize is that in the absence of clearly
stated wishes, their state of residence has a default answer already
provided. The only way to prevent your state from directing your affairs
is by superseding the state's default with your own clear wishes. When
people fail to plan, what they want to happen will rarely occur.

Recent Example

An orthopedic surgeon from Indiana was surprised to learn that his estate plan (we use the term loosely here) would not work the way he thought it would. He and his wife did not think they needed wills because they did not have any children. They were shocked to learn that not everything would go to each other, if one of them died. Rather, their state law dictated that 25% of the deceased person's assets would automatically go to that person's parents–in the absence of a will stating otherwise. This surgeon did not get along with his in-laws, so he was shocked to learn that 25% of his lake home would have gone to them had his wife died. They had put this property in her name alone for asset-protection reasons, not thinking about how this would impact him if she died.[51]

This is not a rare story–we often see doctors and dentists who do not have a proper estate plan established.

> **The first step in building a good plan is to understand the tools available to help your family.**

Wills

A will simply outlines where you want your funds and property to go, and who will raise your minor-age children in the event of your death. The most important issue by far is designating who will raise your children. Some issues to consider when designating a *guardian* are:

- Who would raise your children with similar values to your own?
- With whom could your children make the best transition to life without you?

---

[51]Indiana has since changed this law, but the principle remains the same.

Wills cannot outline how, when, or for what purposes your money should be given to your beneficiaries. This is a major problem with wills as they relate to families with young children. If only a will is used, funds must be dispersed to your children at an age mandated by your state, which is 18 or 21 in most states.

Recent Example
Doug and Amy have the following assets:
- *A $650,000 401(k) account*
- *Home equity of $395,000*
- *Life insurance of $4,500,000*
- *Other miscellaneous assets of $500,000*

Total assets of $6,045,000

Doug and Amy do not currently have a will. Therefore, their children would stand to inherit $6,045,000 at age eighteen if both Doug and Amy die (assuming no estate taxes).

The couple in the example above has a common problem—a large amount of assets, due especially to their life insurance. They know they do not want their children to inherit millions at age eighteen, but they do not know of alternatives. Fortunately the solution is simple.

A Trust for Your Children's Benefit
By establishing a trust for your children's benefit, you can designate how, when, and for what purposes your children should receive the proceeds from your estate. This is your chance to share your values as a family through your estate-planning documents.

A well-respected estate-planning attorney once told us:

People would do well to consider how they plan to parent, should they live, and have their documents accomplish similar objectives, should they not.

This is well put. Unfortunately, the boiler-plate document that many attorneys use with their clients simply distributes the funds at a certain age, with no other thought given to the parent's values for the family. This is one of the important reasons why we suggest our clients use an attorney that specializes in estate planning to draft their documents.

Recent Example

A physician's trust designated that his children were to each receive half of their funds at age 25 and the other half at age 30. When we asked the client his plan for giving money to his children if he was still alive, he had no intention of giving his children a million dollars simply for turning 25 years old.

You have at least three valid options for deciding how to leave money to minor children:

1. Take the normal approach, leaving 1/3 of your money to your kids at three different age intervals (example, 1/3 at age 25, 1/3 at 30, and 1/3 at age 35). Attorneys have said that the concept is: Your children may spend the first 1/3 *before* they get it, the second third the day they get it, and they may never spend the last 1/3.

2. Alternatively, if you have someone you trust completely, you could designate that person as a *trustee* of the funds, and give them full discretionary authority over the money. In other words, you are putting them in the position as a replacement parent in terms of helping with financial decisions for your children.

3. The third option is what is sometimes known as an *incentive trust*. The idea behind an incentive trust is that you provide financial incentive to your children for the things that you valued as a parent, and would have encouraged had you still been living.[52]

---

[52] A well-drafted incentive trust provision must address numerous variables and practical problems, and the final product can and should differ based upon each grantor's specific objectives.

Recent Examples

Attorney Adam Kirwan put a provision in his children's trust document that says their trust will match whatever income they earn from their job. In other words, if they work at Burger King, they may get paid only $10,000 per year from their trust, whereas if they work as a physician, they could get paid hundreds of thousands of dollars per year from their trust. For certain occupations like teaching, he matches 300% of what they earn so there is no disincentive to go into a noble profession that pays less.

Tom Martin, one of this book's authors, has a provision in his children's trusts that gives them money for a down payment on a home. He wants them to be able to afford the other 80% mortgage on their own merit. Tom's trust also provides for his children's education (undergrad and grad school), but they have to maintain a certain GPA in order to keep receiving the funds. If they drop below this GPA, their funding from the trust stops until they get the GPA back to an acceptable level. He and his wife set this up because they did not want to pay for their children to party their inheritance away at college.

One client is a recovering alcoholic. He put a provision in his incentive trust that requires his children to be randomly tested for drug and alcohol use each year. If they fail the test, their inheritance for the year goes to charity.

The point is not that you should use any of the above examples in your own documents. Instead, the point is that these people have all taken the time to put their personal values into place in their documents. Unless you have someone you wholly trust to carry out your wishes, this is an approach you should strongly consider.

In addition to incorporating your family values into your estate plan, trusts can also provide strong asset protection of the funds for your children. If drafted properly, the trust can have a "spendthrift provision." This simply means that if your children run into financial problems elsewhere (divorce or bankruptcy for example), the assets inside of their trust should be protected.

However, wills and trusts are not the only basic documents you need to employ. Advanced directives and powers of attorney are also needed.

Advanced Directives

Advanced directive documents outline how you want your health care decisions to be addressed in the event that something happens to you that causes a medical emergency. A part of the health care directives is the HIPPA authorization. Without this authorization, the hospital or doctors are technically forbidden to discuss your health with anyone beside your spouse without prior court approval. Every client needs to implement health information authorizations for their closest loved ones, and make sure that their loved ones have reciprocated these provisions. The advanced directives also provide direction as it relates to end-of-life and life-support decisions.

Multi-generational planning is commonly overlooked when it comes to advanced directives. Do not forget about your parents. Make sure that they have provided you with a proper HIPPA authorization in their document, and vice versa.

Recent Example

A neurosurgeon client provides financial support for his mother. As part of his estate plan, we suggested he be sure that she has established a HIPPA authorization for him, and that he has a copy of her advanced directives. He found out that she had never done any estate planning of her own, so he offered to have this done in coordination with the update he was doing on his own estate plan.

Powers of Attorney

The final basic document is the power of attorney. This document allows your spouse to sign for you in the event that you are unable. The Marine Corps requires a soldier to sign a power of attorney for his or her spouse before deploying to war. Without this authorization, a spouse's decision-making power is limited on behalf of the other person.

Powers of attorney can either be "durable" or "springing." When a durable power of attorney is in place, it can be used at any time for any purpose designated by the document. A springing power takes effect only in the event of incapacity–when the power of attorney "springs" into action.

Attorneys have their own thoughts on why someone should establish durable or springing powers. Our position is that physicians should weigh the issues of both with help from their attorney, and decide for themselves which one is best suited for their family's situation.

The Financial Impact of Estate Planning

The estate tax, or the death tax as it is also known, is imposed as a means to confiscate wealth so that not too much wealth is passed from one generation to the next. It was originally imposed as a tax only temporarily during war times–once a war was over, the tax was repealed until a new war began. Things changed after World War I though. This time, the tax stayed when the battle ended. At its historical maximum, this tax has confiscated up to 77% of a family's wealth at the death of the second spouse. [66]

Over the past several years, the amount of a physician's wealth that has been subject to estate taxation has been on the constant move. This will oversimplify things, but from a conceptual standpoint:

2002
A physician could pass on $1 million free of estate taxes, and anything above this amount was taxed at approximate 50%.

2002-2009
The amount that could be passed free from estate taxes climbed gradually from $1 million to $3.5 million. The tax rate also declined during this same period from 50% to 45%. By 2009, a physician could pass on $3.5 million free of estate taxes, and anything above this amount was taxed at approximate 45%.

2010
The estate tax was repealed for one year, but in a way that increased taxes for the of many business owners, land owners, and farmers.[53]

---

[53] Due to the elimination of the step-up in basis.

2011-2012

Beginning on January 1, 2011, the estate tax law was scheduled to revert back to the prior 2002 law. Instead, Congress met on December 17, 2010 and passed the Tax Relief, Unemployment Insurance Reauthorization, and Job Creation Act of 2010. This act modified some key provisions of the estate tax for the years 2011 and 2012. It now allows for married couples to pass on $10 million with anything above this amount taxed at approximately 35%.[54]

2013

Unless the law is changed again, we are currently scheduled to revert back to the 2002 law on January 1, 2013. At that point, without any planning in place to avoid it, anything over $1 million will again be taxed at approximately 50%.

Thank you for keeping this simple, Congress! (Please note our sarcasm here).

What Does This Mean for You?

First, the good news is that you do not have to worry about this as it relates to passing money to your spouse as long as you are both U.S. citizens. If not, refer to the advanced planning section in this chapter on page 136. Congress has granted an unlimited exemption to the amount of funds that U.S. spouses can pass to one another without owing any death taxes.

The problem comes when you want to pass wealth to someone other than your U.S.-citizen spouse. In this instance, you can use the following formula to calculate the estate taxes your heirs would have to pay:

2011-2012 Estate Tax Formula

(Your net worth + your life insurance - $10 million) x 35%

(assumes a married couple)

2013 Estate Tax Formula

(Your net worth + your life insurance - $1 million) x 50%

---

[54] $5 million if single.

So, if someone had a net worth of $2 million, and $3 million in life insurance, they would currently owe nothing in federal estate taxes. Suddenly on January 1, 2013, they will owe $2.2 million in death taxes if no estate planning is completed, and the law remains unchanged.

Because this tax would confiscate so much wealth if left unchecked, an entire field of work has been developed in order to help minimize these taxes through any legal means possible. Numerous planning strategies have been created in order to minimize these taxes through creative planning. Some of the more common strategies include:

- Family Limited Partnerships (FLP)
- Qualified Personal Residence Trusts (QPRT)
- Qualified Terminable Interest Property Trusts (QTIP)
- Charitable Lead Trusts (CLT)
- Charitable Remainder Trusts (CRAT and CRUT)
- Intentionally Defective Grantor Trusts (IDGT)
- Dynasty Trusts

The problem with the above strategies for many couples under age sixty-five is that they are not very flexible, if at all, and most require the user to give up a measure of control over their wealth. On top of these problems, some of the above strategies have been flagged by the IRS for automatic audit and challenge if utilized because they are often abused.

Though many of these strategies can be effective if used properly, we would rarely suggest using any of them until a later point in life. Someone with a $6 million net worth at age sixty-five would be a much better candidate for some of the above strategies than a forty-year old. Following is a list of some of the more flexible strategies that would often be appropriate for a younger family:

Flexible Estate Planning Strategies for Younger Families

- Testamentary Trusts
- Revocable Living Trusts
- Credit Shelter / Marital / A-B / Bypass Trusts
- Irrevocable Life Insurance Trusts (ILIT)
- 529 Plans
- Uniform Transfer to Minors Accounts (UTMA)

Testamentary Trusts

This is one way to implement a trust for your children's benefit, as discussed earlier in this chapter. It is simply a paragraph in your will that designates how, when, and why your children should receive their funds. Testamentary means "at death." A testamentary trust is one that is not established until after you die. There is nothing you need do while living except sign a will stating that this should be established at death. This trust, or an equivalent alternative, is essential for anyone who has young children for all of the reasons previously discussed.

Revocable Living Trust

A living trust is established during your lifetime, but does not necessarily have to be funded until your death. Revocable means that you can change it at anytime. Some estate-planning attorneys use this type of trust as their preferred method for leaving wealth to children. Compared to the Testamentary Trust, a Revocable Living Trust is easier to update, and keeps wealth completely confidential at death. In many attorneys' opinions, a living trust becomes essential anytime you own property or businesses in more than one state.

Credit Shelter Trusts

Also known as A-B trusts, marital trusts, or bypass trusts, credit shelter trusts effectively double the amount of assets you can pass on free from death taxes. For example, when the 2013 law says you can pass $1 million of assets with no taxes, using a credit shelter trust might allow you to pass $2 million of assets tax free. At a tax rate of 50%, having this trust in place could save as much as $500,000 in death taxes.[55]

Disclaimer Provisions in Wills

By inserting disclaimer provisions in your will, you can accomplish the same thing as the Credit Shelter (A/B) Trust described above. A disclaimer provision gives your spouse the right to disclaim some of his or her inheritance from you, and put it in trust instead. This effectively accomplishes the same end as the Credit Shelter Trust. The good part is that it gives more options to the surviving spouse than the trust avenue

---

[55]The need for credit shelter trusts was partially eliminated for the years 2011-2012 due to a provision that automatically provides for the doubling of the exemption for married individuals.

does. The bad part is that it gives more options to the surviving spouse–and, therefore, gives him or her more room to make more mistakes.

With the estate tax law in year-by-year flux, many younger physicians are electing to have disclaimer language inserted into their wills, as this gives them the most flexibility in their estate plan, without having to incur the expense or complications of establishing a trust at the current time.

This only solves your full 2013 problem if your estate, including life insurance, is *valued between $1 million and $2 million*. Most physicians have bigger problems if the 2002 standard reappears in 2013. If your estate is valued over this amount, additional planning must be done, or estate taxes will still be owed.

Irrevocable Life Insurance Trusts (ILITs)

The ILIT is often a good solution for our young doctors whose death-tax issues are caused primarily through their ownership of life insurance. Through the ILIT strategy, a trust actually owns your term life insurance policies. When you die, the proceeds from your term life insurance go into a trust for your spouse's and/or children's benefit, likely with zero estate taxes owed on the death benefit amount.

This type of planning is traditionally used with older retirees who acquire permanent death benefits as a means to foot their death tax bill. The twist for young families is in acquiring term (temporary) life insurance in the trust, instead of a permanent death benefit. It is not uncommon for physicians to have more than $5 million of life insurance benefits. By utilizing term (temporary) insurance, a $5 million death benefit usually has a price tag of around $2,000 to $4,000 per year–a very reasonable price to pay for some meaningful protection for your family.[56] For families with assets that are not liquid, like a family business or real estate holdings, an ILIT can also provide necessary funds. With life insurance in place through the ILIT, your estate has cash to pay your death tax bill so that your children do not have to sell your assets in a fire sale to pay the taxes.

The decision on whether to fund an ILIT with temporary life insurance coverage or permanent life insurance coverage depends on several factors. At some point, permanent coverage typically becomes the

---

[56]Assuming a "Standard" health rating or better.

most cost-effective method of funding the death tax. A good analysis will calculate the rate of return you would have to earn on investments outside of the ILIT in order to generate the same after-tax benefit achieved from the life insurance inside the ILIT. If a high rate of return is required, permanent coverage may be the best solution for your dollars, but, in this circumstance, you would want a guaranteed death benefit with the least cost possible. This can often be accomplished by acquiring coverage that requires both spouses to die before it pays a benefit.

529 Plans

As previously discussed on page 104, 529 plans are education savings accounts that can be used to benefit your children. From an estate planning perspective, it is an excellent tool because the proceeds in the account are fully under your control, but are not considered a part of your estate if you die.

If you are married, you can gift up to $130,000 *per child* to a 529 plan without owing a gift tax or without utilizing any of your lifetime exemption. This is also a strategy that wealthy grandparents can implement for their grandchildren, as gifts to 529 plans under the $130,000 amount are often free of generation-skipping taxes.[57]

UTMA Accounts

Uniform Transfer to Minors Accounts can be beneficial in small doses. Through a UTMA, you are eligible to gift up to $26,000 per year per child to an account that remains under your control until your child reaches age eighteen or twenty-one.[58/59] Once the funds have been gifted, they are out of your estate, and are therefore no longer subject to death taxes. Your children also pay a lower capital gains rate on the growth within their account than you would if the funds were still in your name.

A downside of UTMA accounts, however, is that once your child reaches the age of maturity in your state, he can do whatever he wishes with the money, and you no longer have legal rights over the account. We know of one example where the parents had gifted over $100,000 to be used

---

[57]Remember that the full $130,000 value would not be fully removed from the value of the estate (in terms of calculating estate taxes owed) until the fifth year is reached. $130,000 is the 2012 limit.

[58]If married, $26,000; $13,000 if single. 2012 limits.

[59]Depending on your state of residence.

for college education, but once the child reached the maturity age, he neglected his parents' wishes, and instead used the funds for an extended backpacking trip in Europe.

Which Strategies are Appropriate in Your Situation?

The answer depends on your objectives. If your desire is to have a trust that designates how, when, and why your children receive their funds, a testamentary trust, revocable living trust, or an irrevocable life insurance trust (ILIT) could be appropriate. Your assets would help dictate which of these methods would be best for you.

If, instead, your objective is to reduce the estate taxes you owe, credit shelter trusts, disclaimer provisions, 529 plans, or UTMAs may be more appropriate. In many situations, a physician will implement two or more of these strategies to accomplish multiple objectives.

Multi-Generational Planning

One of the highest honors a financial advisor can receive is the opportunity to work with three or four generations within the same family. This speaks volumes about the family's trust in the advisor, but it also bodes well for the family, as it often leads to additional wealth if planning is coordinated across the generations.

Take for example the idea of college funding. It may be possible that your parents could help solve their own estate tax problem by making large gifts to 529 plans for each of their grandchildren. If you turned around and gifted your own funds to a 529 account, you might end up with too much money available that your children will never use. This is a big problem. Any growth in the account above what is needed for education purposes for your children would be subject to income tax, and an additional 10% penalty if withdrawn. For this and many other reasons, it is often important to make sure that coordinated planning has been accomplished across the generations.

Multi-generational planning is especially important any time a large amount of land or a family vacation home is involved. Several of our clients own large plots of land that they would like to gift to their children. If not addressed properly, this can create difficult challenges.

Non-Citizen Spouses

For many physicians, the doctor, the doctor's spouse, or both are not United States citizens. The impact of this on estate taxes can be drastic without proper planning.

Normally a spouse can inherit an unlimited amount of assets with no taxes owed. With non-citizen spouses, the IRS is concerned that he or she will inherit a U.S. citizen's wealth, and leave the country without paying a death tax. As such, Congress imposes limits on the amount of wealth that can be passed at death to a non-citizen spouse without death taxes owed. Limits are also imposed on what dollar amount of assets can be gifted to a non-citizen spouse each year with no gift taxes being owed–normally a spouse can gift an unlimited gift to the other spouse.

A number of solutions exist to this issue–some simple, and some involving complex trusts. The key is making sure that your advisor is aware of you or your spouse's citizenship status and works accordingly.

> **Note:** *Be very cautious as this is one area where few advisors in the various estate, tax, and financial planning disciplines are properly trained.*

Community Property States

Historically, some states have elected to follow Spanish law, rather than English law as it relates to property ownership in the context of a marriage. The states that follow the Spanish system are known as "community property" states.[67]

The Community Property States:

Arizona, California, Idaho, Louisiana, Nevada, New Mexico, Texas, Washington, and Wisconsin are all community property states. Alaska and Puerto Rico have optional community property laws.

If you live in one of these states, they all have slightly different quirks in their laws, making it essential to work with a good, local attorney who specializes in estate planning to address these issues.[60]

---

[60]Louisiana is a particularly complex state with unique laws. [94]

Recent Example

A neurosurgeon completed a will while finishing residency in California. Next he moved to a non-community property state to join a practice. It was important that he update his will at that point because his assets were treated completely differently in the non-community property state.

Other Advanced Issues

Several other advanced estate-planning strategies exist but are beyond the scope of this book. The important thing to note is that this is an area of planning that simply cannot be ignored, or your state and the IRS will make most of the decisions for you. You do not want this to happen.

PRACTICAL APPLICATION

If you have not yet taken the time to establish a proper estate plan, it is now time to get started. Use the discussion points throughout this chapter and on the following pages to help get you started. Work with your financial team to make sure that all of these issues are being properly addressed.

It is often best to work with an attorney that is recognized as a specialist in the area of law in which you need assistance.

The Larson Law Firm specializes in meeting these needs for physicians and their families. They also have access to a great network of attorneys around the country in event they are not well suited for your situation. Please visit www.rsllawfirm.com.

Estate planning cannot be done properly without coordination with the rest of your financial plan. If tax considerations or asset protection considerations are overlooked, it can be devastating to your plan.

Important: Make sure that someone is helping to quarterback this overall process.

Discussion Starters for Estate Planning

This requires participation from your spouse. Our best advice is to schedule a date night out to discuss some of these important issues over dinner. Go through these questions, and have a list of answers ready for your attorney. Then seek your attorney's input on implementing these ideas into your plan.

If you have young children:

- Who would you want to raise your children if you cannot? What if this person is not available? Who is your alternative?
- Do any of your children have any special behavioral or health challenges?
- If while living, you had $2 million to give to each of your children, how would you do it? Should this be different if you die? If so, what would you change?
- Is there anyone you trust completely with your children's financial future? If not, has your advisor recommended a bank or trust company to serve as the trustee of your assets, should something happen to you?

Other issues to address:

- Do your children have needs that cannot be met on their own? Will leaving your assets to your children help or harm them?
- Is there a certain piece of property, vacation home, or family retreat that you want to make sure is kept in the family?
- Do you own real estate in multiple states?
- Do you have any concerns about the stability of any of your children's marriages?
- Who would you want to manage your family's investments if something happened to you?
- Do you have HIPPA documentation signed and accessible by your appropriate loved ones?
- Is there anyone that you would want to have access to important health information, outside of your spouse and minor children? A parent? A grown child?

- Are there any charities you are currently supporting that you would like to continue supporting in death?
- Would you be willing to use at least $1 million of your assets to establish a family foundation today to carry out your charitable endeavors?

Financial issues to consider:
- Do you have any highly appreciated assets?
- Is your net worth, including life insurance benefits, over $1 million? If so, have you taken steps to solve your potential estate/death tax problems?
- Are you or your spouse *not* a U.S. citizen?
- Is asset protection of extreme importance to you?

Take your answers when you meet with your attorney who will have other questions for you to consider, but this will be a good starting point in your discussions.

For further reading:
- *Disinherit the IRS*, by E. Michael Kilbourn
- *Family Wealth,* by James E. Hughes, Jr.
- *Splitting Heirs: Giving Money & Things to Your Children Without Ruining their Lives*, by Ron Blue and Jeremy White
- *Tools & Techniques of Estate Planning*, by Leimberg, et al
- *Beating the Midas Curse*, by Cochell and Zeeb

CHAPTER 8

Asset Protection Planning
Beat a Lawsuit Before It Begins

---

*"Don't wear yourself out trying to get rich. Be wise enough
to know when to quit. In the blink of an eye wealth disappears,
for it will sprout wings and fly away like an eagle."*
Proverbs 23:4 [3]

A surgeon was driving in the parking lot at one of the world's most
prestigious teaching hospitals. He had just spent a long day in the O/R
working on an especially difficult case, and was running late for his
daughter's spelling bee. As he rushed through the parking lot on his way
to the school, he accidentally struck a nurse who was walking to her
vehicle. He got out of the car to make sure she was all right. She had a
few minor scrapes on her legs, and said she was okay other than that.
He walked her to her car, and even called her the next day just to make
sure she was still okay. He was told that she was just fine and that there
were no problems. Two weeks later he received notice of a civil lawsuit.
Apparently she had checked herself in to the emergency room three days
after the accident occurred. He learned through a friend of a friend that
she had been urged by her colleagues to "go after the easy money."

Asset Protection Defined
While the estate planning process focuses on preventing many different
wealth-eroding factors (taxes, prodigal spenders, poor trust structure,
divorce, and others), for this book's purpose, asset protection is specific
to wealth erosion caused by a liability claim or bankruptcy.

With the advent of Internet
research, asset protection has
become a major concern for
physicians. Today it is possible
that for less than $1,000, others
can easily uncover the following
information about you: [68]

- Your annual income and the
  income of your spouse
- Your assets
- Your social security number
- The balance in your accounts
- The location of your accounts,
  including account numbers
  and safe deposit boxes
- The investment positions you own, and the trades you have placed in
  your accounts
- The equity in your home
- Your mother's maiden name

> "Many advisors give lip service to asset protection in their planning, but our experience is that few advisors do more than use this topic as a means to sell more products."

Based on the above information, a plaintiff's attorney can quickly tell
if you are a good candidate to be a defendant in his lawsuit. If you have
deep pockets, great income, and a lot of assets, it is far more likely you
will find yourself on the wrong end of a lawsuit. On the other hand, if a
little research uncovers that you only own a home with little equity and
few other assets in your name, you are much more likely to avoid the
unpleasantness and expense of a lawsuit.

We are frequently asked about asset protection in specific relationship
to medical malpractice issues. As a result, we have compiled the
following data to show the trends and breakdown of near-term
malpractice claims history by state.[61]

---

[61] 2007 Medical Malpractice Crisis States, as determined by the American Medical Association, cross-referenced with information from the 2007 Kaiser Family Foundation analysis of data from the National Practitioner Data Bank (NPDB). States are listed in order of highest average claims first. For further information on the current state of medical reforms: http://www.ama-assn.org/resources/doc/arc/mlr-now.pdf

Ranking of State Malpractice Concerns

AMA Crisis States	Relatively Large Average Claims	Relatively Large Total Claims
Wyoming	✔	
Illinois	✔	✔
Massachusetts	✔	✔
Conneticut	✔	
New York	✔	✔
New Jersey	✔	✔
Pennsylvania	✔	✔
Kentucky	✔	
Nevada	✔	
Ohio	✔	✔
North Carolina		✔
Oregon		
Washington		✔
Florida		✔
Tennessee		
Rhode Island		
Missouri		✔

Unfortunately, some physicians erroneously consider the need for asset protection only in the context of medical malpractice. Although malpractice claims are a legitimate concern in several high-risk states, our experience is that malpractice should not be the sole focus or main concern. Anecdotally, we have witnessed several physicians sued for frivolous malpractice issues, but we have yet to personally see one lose a dime of their own money to a malpractice claim. However, we have seen several examples where physicians had their personal assets successfully attacked as a result of a claim outside of their medical practice.

We became even more passionate about this issue after a good friend of one of our advisors lost his multimillion-dollar nest egg due to a frivolous injury lawsuit caused by someone else. He was the only one with deep pockets in the vicinity of the event, so the attorneys went after him–and won. This entire family was hit hard emotionally, and his net worth was decimated from $8 million to $350,000. This cemented our opinion that this is an important area of comprehensive wealth management that doctors and dentists simply cannot afford to ignore.[62]

When it comes to asset protection, timing is everything. In fact there are only two timeframes: before and after a hint of trouble. Carefully constructed asset protection strategies that are fully implemented before any hint of trouble are much more likely to succeed, and can save you hundreds of thousands, or even millions, of dollars. By "hint of trouble," we mean before an event occurs that could trigger a lawsuit, or long before it appears that your creditors may push you into bankruptcy.

Unfortunately, the same is not true for asset protection strategies initiated *after a hint of trouble.* Moving assets to avoid existing plaintiffs or creditors could cause major problems, and leave you subject to a claim of fraudulent conveyance. This could cause you to automatically lose your suit; in the worst-case scenario, you could go to jail. This is the key message: the sooner you get started, the more likely you will be able to protect you and your family from losing your assets to litigation. We believe the best strategy for physicians who want to protect their assets is to take a two-pronged approach:

Step One: Avoid situations that put you at risk. In other words, avoid lawsuits in the first place. This could mean avoiding dangerous situations and minimizing risk.

Step Two: Make it so difficult for plaintiffs to sue you and recover that they don't bother to go after you in the first place, even if an event does occur. The result: Your assets and your business are protected and prevented from claims if you are sued. In other words, with a carefully drafted plan, your plaintiffs will not have an economic incentive to sue you.

It is estimated that over 19 million lawsuits will be filed in the U.S. this year.[68] The focus of asset-protection planning is to establish appropriate measures ahead of time so that when a lawsuit comes your way, you are already prepared to defend yourself. Many different strategies exist to attempt to protect assets, but the finest are those that do so aboveboard, without trying to hide anything.

---

[62] Particulars are altered to protect the friend's privacy but the story is still very much on point with what happened.

To further explain this concept, it is essential to first understand the anatomy of how a lawsuit functions. We divide a lawsuit into five different stages:

Stage 1: Risk/Reward Analysis
- It typically begins with an unfortunate event where someone is injured–physically, emotionally, or financially.
- An attorney enters the picture, and looks for the "deep pockets" available from which to extract money. As someone with a higher-than-average income or net worth, you are automatically considered a "deep-pocketed target."
- The plaintiff's attorney will hire an information firm to put together a packet containing all of the financial data they can find about you. It will be thorough. Based on this information, the attorney will make a decision about the risk/reward of filing a suit against you. This is a critical moment. You don't even know yet that you are potentially subject to this lawsuit, and the attorney's decision whether or not to go after you will depend on what information he or she can gather about you. It doesn't take much for you to become a viable target, for example, 33% of $100,000 is still $33,333 in fees to the attorney.

Stage 2: The Complaint
- Next the plaintiff's attorney will file a complaint/lawsuit (sometimes a very vague one).
- You will be served with the complaint and a summons. This may be the first moment you know you have a problem on your hands, and you will always be way behind the plaintiff's attorneys as far as strategy. Remember, they already know about your assets, liabilities, spending tendencies, etc.
- In fact, when possible, they will ask the court right up front to issue a Writ of Attachment. This process freezes your access to your assets so that you are not tempted to move them elsewhere–now that you know you have a problem. This is another crucial juncture in the case. If a Writ of Attachment is granted, it will be hard for you to maintain your lifestyle during the course of the trial.

Stage 3: Mounting Your Defense

- You will immediately call your attorney and business manager, if a malpractice issue, to let them know you received a complaint and a summons. The attorney will charge you an upfront retainer fee for the case, typically in excess of $10,000.
- The attorney helping with your liability issue may not have a good handle on asset protection issues, so you will need to hire a second attorney to help you make sense of what is at stake, based on the first attorney's recommendations for how the case should be handled.
- If a malpractice issue, you may also have to hire an attorney to fight your malpractice carrier if they are seeking to settle a case where you are not at fault. If they settle the case, your record will have a major blemish–but they may only consider the lowest possible financial loss.[63]
- The type of litigation you are facing, and your state of residence, will determine what your options are from a defense standpoint.
- While your legal team sorts through your options, the opposing attorneys will request a mountain of paperwork from you. It will take you out of production for hours on end. They already know most of what you have, but they will ask you to gather everything possible about your financial life. You will feel like your privacy is being violated, without realizing that it was already violated a long time ago when the plaintiff's attorneys were looking at your account details without your knowledge.
- Next the opposing/plaintiff's attorney will want to meet with you to go over the paperwork in detail. The entire objective of this meeting is to gather as much dirt as possible about your private life. They will ask about the things you would never talk about with anyone, and you will need to answer these questions truthfully or be subject to "contempt of court."
- Often the plaintiff's attorneys will subject you to medical and psychiatric evaluations to see if anything pops up that they can use against you. By this point, you will feel that you have zero privacy remaining in your life.
- They will ask to view all of your computer files to see if your emails, the websites you visit, or your files can give them any additional ammo to use against you.

---

[63] See page 43 for a better understanding of the "hammer clause" in malpractice insurance.

- Part of the strategy you will have to work through with your attorney will be determined by what you actually have to lose. In some states, you will work as hard as possible with your attorneys to posture yourself for quick bankruptcy filing in the event the suit is lost. In other states, you will do everything possible to avoid bankruptcy because state laws will be friendlier to you than Federal bankruptcy statutes.

Stage 4: The Trial
- Your attorney will try to get things settled before a jury trial ever occurs because many jurors will likely have minimal knowledge of the complex medical issues involved, which could diminish your chances of winning at trial.
- If the case does not get settled, and you go to court and win, you will still be out the time and money it cost you to get to this point. Only under rare circumstances will the judge demand the plaintiff pay your attorney's fees.
- Worse, if the case does not get settled, and you lose the case–even if you were not in the wrong–the opposition will get a judgment against you, and act quickly to seize control of your assets. The amount of the judgment will be determined in large part by how the judge or jury *feels* about you and about the plaintiff. Attorney Robert Mintz states, "Judges and juries often act on their emotions–not on the law." [68]

Stage 5: Appeals and Collection
- The entire process will have been mentally draining on your family up until this point. It will feel unfair every step of the way, and the very core of your dignity will feel it has been violated. With this much additional stress, your personal relationships will also suffer.
- With few assets left available, you will have little financial strength remaining to mount an appeal unless your friends or family are willing to foot the bill to help you fight a battle you have already lost once. This is because in order to appeal the case, you will be required to obtain a bond that promises to pay the original verdict if you cannot later. In order to obtain this bond, you will need to have *cash* available *in excess* of the original judgment against you to provide proper collateral for the bond.
- In order to satisfy the judgment against you, you will be forced to settle the case, pay the judgment, or file bankruptcy. If a settlement

is not agreeable, your attorney will fight to use either the state or Federal laws to help you (whichever is best), while the opposing legal team will seek to get the opposite set of rules applied to your situation, because this is better for them and the plaintiff.

- By now you are running out of options and cash, so your attorney will become less and less helpful because he or she will not want to work for free.
- If you get lucky, the judgment or bankruptcy will be discharged quickly, with no garnishment to your future wages.
- If you are not lucky, you will be starting your financial life completely over–and 25% to 50% of every paycheck you receive will go to pay back the remaining portion of the verdict against you, until it is completely satisfied.
- If you are in private practice, and your medical practice was not set up correctly, you will have to renegotiate all contracts with insurance carriers. You will also have to complete new credentialing with all hospitals where you work.
- In many states you'll be forced to sell your home in order to raise capital to cover the judgment against you. The assets that remained protected will be those that are not very liquid, so you will have to start over from scratch rebuilding your family's financial life.

Does the above sound too absurd to happen to your family?

We are amazed by some of the verdicts that have been handed out by juries and judges in our own communities, and even more amazed by some of the judgments handed out around the country. Randy Cassingham gives out The True Stella Awards®[64] each year for the most wild, outrageous, or ridiculous lawsuits. He states in his book, *The True Stella Awards*,[69] "Other times, people view doctors and hospitals more as deep pockets full of money than as partners in responsible health care." Based on the following ridiculous cases, it is clear that anything is possible when a creative plaintiff's attorney gets involved.

The Stella Awards® are named after Stella Liebeck. Most can recall the 1992 McDonald's®[65] case where a woman was awarded $2.86 million dollars for spilling hot coffee on herself. [69]

---

[64] Stella Awards® is a registered trademark of This is True, Inc.
[65] McDonald's is a registered trademark of McDonald's.

In 1992, an intoxicated woman backed her car into the local bay and drowned. Her parents sued the Japanese auto manufacturer for making a seatbelt that could not be opened by a legally intoxicated person underwater–and won $65 million dollars. [70]

In Hawaii, a car struck a minor on the sidewalk when the driver passed out due to a new medication he was taking. The parents of the minor sued the physician for improperly prescribing the medicine. The Supreme Court of Hawaii decided for the first time that a physician could indeed be liable for a personal injury caused to a third party by a patient. [71]

In Colorado, a prankster put glue on a toilet seat at a home improvement store. The man who was hurt by the prank filed suit against the store demanding $3 million dollars. [72]

In Rolling Fork, Mississippi a patient sued her physician for prescribing a drug that had become part of a class-action lawsuit. The patient admitted she was never hurt by the drug, and had only sued because she thought, "I might get a couple of thousand dollars." The physician and his wife, another physician, packed up and left the state as a result of the lawsuit. The whole town suffered because these two physicians represented 50% of all doctors in town. [69]

The case that leaves the worst taste in our mouths is the 1997 case where a man was electrocuted by an alarm system while trying to rob a local tavern. The robber's family sued the bar–and won. [73]

Cases like the above demonstrate that asset protection is important for any physician with substantial assets or income. Asset protection attorney Robert Mintz warns, "Every day in court a sympathetic plaintiff prevails against a wealthy or comparatively wealthy defendant–even in those cases which appear to be absurd, illogical, and utterly without merit." [68]

You have worked way too hard to see your efforts go up in smoke because they were not properly protected.

The biggest problem with asset protection: It is an ever-evolving discipline. Once a strategy is used frequently, an attorney somewhere finds a way to beat it. What works, and does not work, is also different on a state-by-state basis, as every state has different laws to circumvent. To ensure your assets are as safe as possible, it is important to work with an expert attorney who specializes in asset protection to make sure that your plan is up to date with the most recent case law.

What Asset Protection is Not

Asset protection is *not* about trying to hide your assets or evade taxes. It is also *not* reactive. If you are already in the middle of a lawsuit, it is too late to employ most of the strategies discussed below. Instead, asset protection is about being proactive and structuring your assets to be as safe as possible *before* the event occurs that causes the need to protect them.

It seems that every few months another scam artist comes out with a new asset-protection strategy that promises you will not owe any more taxes, or that it is completely "bullet proof." Our experience is that people purchasing these protection packages pay thousands of dollars for a boilerplate trust that does absolutely nothing to reduce their taxes or protect their assets.

Before we discuss legitimate strategies to protect your assets, here are some strategies that are abusive, or have become obsolete.

Strategies to Avoid:
- Offshore trusts to evade taxes
- 419 plans (in most cases)
- Trying to hide assets in Nevada corporations
- Family Limited Partnerships (FLPs) purely for asset-protection purposes
- Limited Liability Companies with no business purpose
- Almost anything done after a lawsuit is already imminent
- Many "asset-protection" trusts

Each of these strategies has inherent problems. Remember that the intent is not to defraud anyone or hide anything. To the contrary, you want to be able to walk into the settlement meeting with a full net-worth statement, and have your attorney strategically show the opposition's attorney everything you own. You want their mouths to drop wide open in despair when they realize that even if they win, they will not be able to get their hands on most of your assets. You want them in a position where they have little choice but to drop the suit, or settle for pennies on the dollar.

> ## In fact, the best asset protection planning is never about asset protection.

Instead, asset protection planning is all about telling a good story to a judge or jury–a story that ultimately makes you look good in court. In *The Asset Protection Guide for Florida Physicians*, Adam O. Kirwan, J.D., LL.M. shares the example of a Florida asset-protection case where the physician kept his assets because he was able to tell a truthful story to the judge about setting his assets up in the way he did because he had been working with a financial planner for years. The judge liked the story so the client kept his assets.[19]

The whole process is much harder for physicians since the passage of the Bankruptcy Abuse Prevention and Consumer Protection Act of 2005. This law made it much more difficult for physicians to protect their hard-earned assets because it made it prohibitive for most physicians to claim a Chapter 7 bankruptcy.

Asset Protection Strategies

In today's environment, assets can legitimately be protected through six general strategies:

1. Acquire insurance to pay creditor claims, instead of you paying.
2. Hold exempt assets that are protected by law from the claims of creditors.
3. Title assets to strategically limit your liability.
4. Un-bundle assets into multiple entities and/or jurisdictions so that they are more difficult to attack.
5. Strip equity away from those assets that are easily attacked.
6. Maintain privacy and a low profile so that you are not seen as someone with "deep pockets" worth pursuing.

Insurance for Asset Protection

Liability insurance is often the best first line of defense in protecting your assets against a claim. Some proponents disagree and suggest that having meaningful amounts of insurance can actually cause you to become the target of a lawsuit. This logic may be true if the physician has an ultra-high net worth, has assets well protected, and lives in the right state. But provided those criteria are not met, insurance is often the most cost-effective way to provide a first line of asset protection defense.

Basic Liability Coverage

Homeowner's insurance and auto insurance provide the most basic forms of liability coverage. Auto insurance covers most claims arising from the use of your automobiles. Homeowner's insurance covers personal liability in general, whether it involves your home or not. Relatively speaking, the insurance coverage provided by these policies is minimal. It is essential to supplement these policies with an umbrella liability insurance policy.

Umbrella Liability Insurance

Umbrella liability insurance sits on top of your auto and homeowner's insurance coverage. It provides additional protection above and beyond the small amounts of coverage provided by your basic coverage. For example, if your auto insurance coverage provides only $500,000 of liability coverage, it is usually possible to acquire $5 million or more additional coverage to sit on top of this policy. This coverage protects many forms of liability that arise from your personal activities, but does not provide any protection for business or professional activities.

Business Liability Coverage

Basic business liability coverage is designed to protect the claims that arise as a result of normal business activities outside of the professional realm. For example, a claim arising because a patient slipped on your office floor would be insured through business liability insurance.

Medical Malpractice Insurance

Malpractice coverage comes in many forms, but exists to protect someone in a professional role against the claims arising from a patient or client that feels wrongly treated.

Malpractice coverage is important to hold, but it can also be the cause of lost assets. With malpractice insurance, the insurance company only has a limited amount of risk at stake (the policy limits), whereas the physician has unlimited financial risk beyond the liability limits. An insurance company may be motivated to take a risk in court, knowing the maximum of funds at stake. This does nothing to protect the professional's financial risk though. Alternatively, the insurance company may prefer to settle the case with no regard for how this might impact your professional record or ability to continue to practice your specialty. For these reasons, it is essential for a doctor to consult with his or her own independent attorney any time a malpractice claim arises.[66]

Note: *Read a further explanation of Medical Malpractice Insurance options on page 39.*

Officers and Directors Liability

Although this coverage falls under the broader scope of professional liability coverage, many people forget to check out the charitable boards on which they serve. In the wake of corporate scandals in the past five years, laws have become stricter on the responsibilities held by directors of companies–whether for-profit or not-for-profit. We suggest that anyone serving on a charitable board should make sure that the board maintains adequate director's and officer's liability coverage.

Exempt Assets for Asset Protection

Exempt assets are those assets that are typically excluded from a judgment or bankruptcy by state or federal law. Even if you lose a lawsuit, you should be able to keep those assets you hold, which are exempt from the claims. Although this can vary widely on a state-by-state and type-of-case basis, some commonly exempt assets include:
- The equity in a personal residence
- Retirement accounts
- Education funding accounts
- Life insurance account values
- Annuity account values

Home Equity

The equity you hold in your home may or may not be an exempt (protected) asset, depending on your state of residence. For example, Missouri protects only $15,000 of home equity for a family, whereas Florida often offers unlimited protection of home equity, provided that someone has lived there for at least 1,215 days (3 years and 4 months) prior to the lawsuit. In a state like Florida, it would be more desirable to

[66]Depending on the state.

pay off one's home because those assets are more likely to be protected. However, in Missouri, it would often be preferable to maintain a large mortgage for as long as possible.

401(k)s, Profit-Sharing, and Pension Plans
401(k) plans, profit-sharing plans, and pensions are typically protected assets. They come with built-in federal asset protection. It has been reported that O.J. Simpson was able to keep an estimated $4.1 million in his retirement plan, even though he lost and could not afford to pay the $30 million civil suit related to the deaths of Nicole Brown Simpson and Ronald Goldman. [74]

IRAs
Individual retirement accounts, though exempt to a certain extent in most states, are not always as well protected as 401(k) accounts. For example, many states do not provide unlimited exemption of IRAs, but instead only exempt a certain dollar amount–often $1 million. This can create a dilemma if you leave an employer, and have a 401(k) plan valued at more than the exempt amount. As a standard recommendation, most investment brokers suggest that you roll over the proceeds of your 401(k) to an IRA account. This might often be wise from an investment perspective, but may not be from an asset-protection standpoint if you are outside the scope of your state's exempted amount. In this case, you may be better off, from a purely asset-protection standpoint, to roll your 401(k) plan into another 401(k) plan at your new employer, instead of moving the funds to an IRA.

Other IRA Arrangements
Roth IRAs and non-deductible IRAs are not as well protected in some states as pre-tax retirement plans. Be careful to learn your state's laws before investing a large portion of your assets in these plans. The discrepancy arises as some states' laws only protect those assets inside of IRA accounts that were federally tax deductible when the contributions were made. This caveat would exclude Roth IRA accounts or non-deductible IRAs that were funded with after-tax dollars.

Education Plans
Education plans and UTMA accounts are exempt in several states. In

some states though, this protection is eliminated for 529 plans if you are the one listed as the owner of the account. Also, 529 plans also have not yet been heavily tested through the courts, so at this point we have to assume that it is safest to fund these accounts well in advance of any claims. A few states specifically offer exemption to their own 529 plans, and although the investment options may not be as strong, this is an issue to consider in determining where to establish your 529 accounts.

Life Insurance Cash Value and Annuities
Life insurance cash values and annuity accounts are afforded liability protection in many states, but not in all states. These tools are important because, if used properly, they provide physicians living in certain states with an easy opportunity for converting non-protected dollars into protected dollars. The problem is that most insurance advisors have no idea what the case law in their client's state dictates, so they go around selling this as a strategy to everyone. Imagine stashing away $3 million dollars into a life insurance policy, only to find that it was not protected at all in your state.

Recent Example

Take for example a physician we encountered living and practicing in Michigan. When contemplating bankruptcy, his original attorney told him his life insurance was not protected. We suggested through his friend (our client) that he should seek a second opinion. It was good that he did because his new attorney, who was a specialist in these matters, clarified for him that it was protected because his beneficiaries were properly established. His new attorney explained to him that life insurance values have twice been beaten as an asset protection strategy in Michigan, but that they should be fully protected in his situation.

Life insurance and annuities offer certain benefits other than asset protection. These other benefits can be found on pages 49, 65, and 68. For this section though, we offer three specific considerations as they relate to using life insurance or annuities for asset protection purposes:

- First, if using life insurance or annuities for asset-protection purposes, make sure that these vehicles are actually protected in your home state.
- Second, understand that these tools have expenses that may not exist with other investments. For example, annuities typically have expenses 1-2% greater per year than their mutual-fund counterparts. If annuities are protected in your state, the question becomes, "Are you comfortable with this added expense in order to gain stronger asset protection?" If the expense for protection is not palatable, annuities may not be an appropriate asset-protection solution for your family.
- Third, be sure the company you are working with has a way to get you your money if you need it during a lawsuit. We know of at least one well-known company that promotes insurance as an asset protection tool, but literally has no process for the insured to get money out of their policy if they ever find themselves in a bankruptcy proceeding caused by a lawsuit. The issue is that this company is only willing to issue a check in the policy owner's name, and not to anyone else designated by the policy owner. Therefore, the creditors would have immediate claim to any check issued to the defendant at the time he needed the cash.

As you can see, potential benefits are available in certain states for using annuities or life insurance for asset-protection purposes, but these benefits must be weighed against the costs. Our recommendation is that life insurance and annuities should rarely be used *only* for asset-protection purposes. Rather, they are better tools if they *also* make sense for reasons outside of asset protection. The asset protection then becomes an added bonus that other solutions might not provide.

Ownership Arrangements
By paying attention to how your assets are owned or titled, you can pick up a measure of asset protection on certain assets in several states.

Joint or Spousal Ownership
Some states offer asset protection for assets either owned jointly with a spouse, or in a spouse's name alone. This strategy only works if your spouse is not a party to the lawsuit. Many instances arise that cause both

spouses to become a party to the suit. Therefore this strategy should be used only on a limited basis in coordination with estate planning and other asset-protection strategies.

We see this strategy used improperly by many physicians who put their home in their spouse's name, believing that this will better protect their personal residence. If you are considering this strategy, be sure to consult with a qualified attorney who knows your state's laws and case history inside and out. It may be more beneficial to own your home jointly by what is known as *tenants by the entirety* than to put it in your spouse's name, but this is very much a state-by-state issue.

Domestic Trusts

A trust can be used to own your assets so that they are not in your own name. Domestic trusts, those established within the U.S., have become the most frequently promoted asset-protection strategy we see. These trusts can come in many different forms (many of which have been described previously in the estate-planning section) and accomplish many different functions. As it relates to asset protection, it is important to know that if you maintain control over the funds inside the trust, these assets are not likely protected–no matter what the attorney selling the trust has to say.

Case law has dictated time and again that judges have little problem compelling defendants to invade trusts that they control in order to satisfy a judgment. Consider the case of the Andersons from San Diego. In this case, and several like it, the defendants transferred their money to a trust to protect it from creditors. The judge simply ordered that the Andersons get the money out of the trust, and use it to pay the judgment. Their defense story was only about asset protection, and the judge was not impressed. [21]

Ironically, one of our advisors recently received a phone call from a resident on the verge of graduation. She wanted to know if she should set up an LLC because one of her attendings told her that she should do this and have the LLC own all of her assets. Little did the attending realize that both the state where they currently work, and the state where this physician is headed, offer little protection of an LLC that is established with no legitimate business purpose.

Near one of our regional offices, a prominent attorney sells Family Limited Partnerships to everyone for asset-protection purposes. High net-worth families pay $10,000 for an "Asset Protection Kit" that provides some instructions on how to answer the fill-in-the-blank forms. The problem: This trust will *do absolutely* nothing to protect these families' assets. Case law in their state already dictates that a Family Limited Partnership is not an asset-protected ownership arrangement, unless 5% or more of the trust is owned by a completely unrelated party. Many of these families have admitted that if they had known they would need to give up control of 5% of their assets to an unrelated party-in order for this strategy to work-they never would have used this strategy.

Offshore Trusts

Physicians ask us many questions about offshore trusts. Maybe the idea sounds exotic. Covert spy fantasies aside, offshore trusts offer pros and cons. Consider the following issues:

There is no debate about it. Offshore trusts can do a great job of protecting assets. Most offshore jurisdictions have laws in place that forbid them from acknowledging a request from a U.S. court to send your money back to satisfy a judgment. The challenge is that historically U.S. judges have not looked favorably on this strategy. The judge's recourse here is to demand that you get the money back, and use it to satisfy the judgment. If you do not comply, the judge has the ability to hold you in contempt, and put you in jail until you agree to comply.
Some famous cases exemplify this:

- This is exactly what occurred in the Anderson case previously mentioned. As a result of this case, holding someone in contempt of court due to their failure to repatriate assets, became known as "Anderson relief."
- In 1997, a failed derivatives trader filed for bankruptcy protection after transferring his assets to a series of offshore trusts. The federal bankruptcy judge declared he was in contempt of court and threw him in prison for several years.

Another issue: Offshore trusts in and of themselves do absolutely nothing to provide any tax savings. Since the passing of the Patriot Act in 2001, most offshore jurisdictions now have treaties in place with the U.S. government to help prevent money laundering and tax evasion. Tax evasion is a criminal offense and can result in jail time. Never listen to anyone who tells you that an offshore trust can be used to evade taxes.

This is not worth the risk.

Some practical issues become apparent with offshore trusts.

- Fees can start at $10,000 to $20,000, and go to $50,000 or more to establish an offshore trust. Make sure your assets justify this kind of expense.
- Be careful to choose the right country and bank to hold your money. Although many offshore companies are trustworthy, and ethical, we have read some examples where an unruly Caribbean banker absconded with the dollars that someone stateside was trying to protect. Make sure you are dealing with a trustworthy, experienced entity.
- *Never* use an offshore trust for the purpose of tax evasion.

Properly drafted offshore trusts can be a great option in the right situation. However, they do not work for everyone. This is an area where an experienced attorney is vital in giving you advice that fits your facts.

Un-bundling of Assets
Multiple Entities
A good strategy is to segregate assets from one another so that any lawsuit could only take a portion of your assets. For example, a medical practice should be a completely different entity than the physician's personal affairs. That way, liability is limited to wherever the incident occurred, and your personal property should be safe if a non-malpractice claim arises in your practice.

The strategy of using multiple entities can sometimes be used to segregate personal assets as well. For example, if a family had a lake home and jet skis, the lake home might be structured into one limited liability company, and the jet skis placed in another. The idea is that if someone is injured while riding on your jet ski, the other assets might be protected.

This strategy was immensely popular a decade ago, but some courts have limited the usage of this strategy for two reasons. First, they have claimed that the company must have a legitimate purpose beyond asset protection. Second, if the ownership is all in your name, some courts have overturned the protective elements.

Today, the safest ways to use the multiple-entities strategy are to have:

- A legitimate purpose for establishing another entity. For example, assuming the above scenario, estate-planning purposes could be used to establish the entity owning the lake home, and a business could be established that rents out the jet skis to others on your lake.
- An unrelated party own a percentage of the interest in the limited-liability companies. This makes it more difficult to claim that the assets are completely under your control.

Multiple Jurisdictions

It often makes sense to use multiple states or countries to establish or hold your assets because this would greatly increase the complexity of going after them. For example, it might make sense to have limited liability companies established in different states that own different facets of your business assets. Why? Every jurisdiction where your assets are held, or entities are established, means that the attorney going after your assets will need to file separate and distinct documents. If the jurisdiction is outside of a state where the attorney is licensed, they will also have to hire local counsel to help them with these filings. All of these issues cost the attorney time and money.

> **Remember that the ultimate goal here is for the attorney to decide that it is not worth the effort to go after you and, instead, find an easier target.**

Using multiple jurisdictions does nothing by itself to protect your assets, but it does help add to the headaches experienced when the attorney realizes that he or she will have to go through multiple proceedings and filings to gain access to your assets.

Equity Stripping

The simple fact is that if you do not have any equity in something, nothing can be taken in a lawsuit or bankruptcy proceeding. Equity stripping is a strategy that leverages debt in order to minimize equity in certain, non-protected assets.[67]

---

[67] Please note: Under certain circumstances, equity stripping can be considered fraud. Make sure you are working with competent legal and tax counsel, and that your actions are being taken prior to any potential claims.

Mortgages

This strategy works well in states where home equity is not well protected. The idea is to mortgage all or a major portion of your home's equity in order to move the funds to a better-protected asset.

Accounts Receivable Factoring

Equity stripping is also used to protect many companies' accounts receivable. For large medical practices in states that do not have caps on damages, outsourcing accounts receivable, or leveraging against it with a loan, can be a great strategy. We have seen some groups take a loan out against their accounts receivable in order to pay off real estate used by the practice, but owned by a different entity. Alternatively, some groups leverage their accounts receivable in order to purchase well-protected assets.

Captive Insurance Companies

Another strategy employed primarily by medical groups is known as a captive insurance company. Through this process, the medical group, or multiple medical groups, establishes its own insurance company to provide medical malpractice insurance. For certain specialties in high-risk states, this can be a very cost-effective solution. It can reduce malpractice premiums drastically, while protecting some of the practice's assets at the same time. Because reinsurance is often used in coordination with this strategy, there is a cap on the damages that must be paid by the captive insurance company.

Keeping a Low Profile

Do not be surprised when some of the previously discussed strategies get challenged in court. Asset protection planning is an ever-evolving process that is never stagnant. What works at the time we wrote this book will not likely work five or ten years from now.

Our advice: Protect your assets as much as possible with the understanding that everything you have done may be challenged if a lawsuit arises. Our experience is that the opposition's attorneys have no qualms about challenging prior case law. The outcome will often be left up to a judge or a jury that has the opportunity to override the prior law.

In addition to using multiple strategies, the best way to *never need them* is to keep a low profile about your wealth, keeping it as private as possible. The best asset-protection strategy of all is to make sure that the bulls-eye never shows up on your back. This is especially challenging any time the letters MD show up after your name, but living a modest lifestyle can head off many predators.

PRACTICAL APPLICATION

As a financial discipline like tax or investment planning, asset protection is new to the menu of services offered to affluent physicians.[21] As a result, asset protection is not yet on the radar of many financial advisors, tax accountants, or estate-planning attorneys.

In the medical industry, we see current trends for malpractice claims, but this is not the only reason for asset protection. Asset protection is an area of complete wealth management doctors cannot afford to ignore. In other words, make sure that your advisors are looking at your plan through asset protection lenses, and that your financial life follows the six fundamental principles outlined in this chapter.

Physicians who are properly protected show little assets worth going after by a plaintiff's attorney because they have made themselves less of a target. In asset protection, timing is everything, with only two timeframes: *before* and *after a hint of a problem.*

Asset protection is not about trying to hide your assets or evade taxes–and it's not reactive. Instead, it is all about telling a good story to a judge or jury. As a result, it is critical to structure your assets according to a well-designed estate, tax, and financial plan *before* the event occurs that causes them to need to be protected. Anything done for the sole purpose of asset protection is suspicious, and might not hold up in court.

You need to get with an expert in this area–and do it soon. If you are not sure with whom to seek counsel, contact us, and we will get you connected with a professional in your area.

For further reading:
- *The Asset Protection Guide for Florida Physicians,* by Adam O. Kirwan, J.D., LL.M.
- *Asset Protection: Concepts & Strategies for Protecting Your Wealth,* by Jay D. Adkisson and Christopher M. Riser
- *Asset Protection for Physicians and High-Risk Business Owners,* by Robert J. Mintz, Esq.

CHAPTER 9

Practice Management
Become a Successful Practitioner and Business Leader

---

*"The truth is that learning how to be a Doctor does not prepare
you to develop a successful medical practice. Knowing how
a practice works best has little to do with knowing how
a Doctor works best."*
Michael E. Gerber, from his book, *The E-Myth Physician* [75]

Little distinguishes one group of private-practice physicians from
another more than their ability to run a business effectively, while also
practicing great medicine at the same time. This can be very difficult
because, unlike dentists and family practice physicians, most specialists
are offered very little in the form of practice management training during
residency or fellowship.

As it relates to the financial side of running a practice, this book isn't
going to focus on hospital administration or the typical Baldrige Criteria
for Performance Excellence. Rather, this book discusses three main
areas of concentration outside of the mainstream practice management
resources:
1. Practice Leadership
2. Profit Maximization
3. Benefits and Compensation

Whether they understand it or not, most physicians today are business
owners, and most of their businesses have a great opportunity in front
of them, regardless of the healthcare laws coming down the pipeline.

Even if you are not a direct owner of a practice, and are an employee of a large institution, the principles outlined in this section should help you become a more effective producer. After reading this chapter, you should have a better handle on the financial fundamentals involved in running a practice well.

Our friend, a large group practice manager, states it correctly when he says that most medical practices are dysfunctional. [76] As this section on practice management unfolds, we will discuss practice leadership, profit maximization, and physician compensation. The following chapter discusses employee benefits from the viewpoint of a practice.

Practice Leadership

Leading a practice in today's environment is like paddling a canoe against choppy waves. The reality is that any business faces ongoing challenges.

> **Business is a game that can only be played, but never won.**

Practice leaders too often forget this statement. Leading a practice through these choppy waters requires six specific disciplines:
1. Integrity
2. Long-term vision
3. Transferring the vision
4. The right people
5. Communication
6. Strategic time

Integrity

The number one problem we observe in some medical practices is a lack of overall integrity.
- Does your practice consistently and dependably do what it says it will do?
- Do your people do what they say they will do?
- And do you personally do what you say you will do?

We all make commitments to ourselves and to others every day. In fact, most days we make dozens or hundreds of such commitments. One of the important differentiators between those physicians that feel excited by the outcomes of their day, and those who feel worn out, is whether or not they kept their commitments. The concept is simple, but once someone makes it a priority, the change is shocking. Consider this example from a typical day:

Recent Example

A Day of Not Keeping Commitments

Dr. Jones plans to take a jog in the morning, but is too tired from being on call last night. He wakes up late, and in his haste, he neglects breakfast. He walks in the door at his office ten minutes late, causing all of his consults to run behind. Because he's running late, he avoids the conversation he needs to have with his scheduler about better protecting his family time.

He grabs some quick food from the physicians' lounge instead of eating the healthier lunch he had planned. He finally gets finished with his patient visits an hour later than anticipated, and rushes directly to his son's soccer game. His wife is upset with him for arriving at the game so late. He's been telling himself he needs to user kinder words with his wife, but her lack of understanding is too much, so he lets his frustration show.

After the soccer game, he rushes back to the office for a business meeting. At the business meeting, he is called on to give a report in response to a question raised at the last meeting. Due to his heavy schedule, he is unprepared. He apologizes to his colleagues, and lets them know he will get it sent out to them by email as soon as he can. On his way home for the night, he checks his voicemail. He has a message from his attorney asking if he's had a chance to review the draft copies of the wills he sent over three months ago.

By the time he walks in the door, he's too frustrated and exhausted by his day to give any of the attention his wife and children want and need.

Unfortunately, similar stories are all too familiar for busy medical professionals. This is a tough, but essential, issue to examine. The most important quality of a good leader, and a good doctor, is integrity–consistently and dependably doing what you say you will do. This process begins in our personal lives. If you or your colleagues do not have personal integrity, it is very difficult to develop corporate integrity. Sloppiness with your word at home inevitably leads to sloppiness with your word at the office and vice versa.

The most difficult aspect of this concept is accountability; it is very difficult to accurately examine one's own actions. We are acutely aware of others' lack of integrity with their word, but we often ignore our own lack because we know of our good intentions. To overcome this hurdle both personally and professionally, we suggest the following:

1. **Become aware of the commitments you make**
   What commitments are you making to others and to yourself throughout the day?
   Are you aware of the commitments you make about:
   - How you will spend your morning?
   - When you will exercise?
   - What you will eat?
   - Who you will return emails or calls from, and when?
   - When you will see patients?
   - When you will be home?
   - How you will treat your spouse or children?
   - What you will do for your practice?

   Chances are that you may be making dozens of commitments everyday that you currently take for granted.

2. **Take the nebulousness out of your commitments**
   Confusion results from nebulous commitments. Have you ever received an email from someone saying "I'll get back to you on that issue."? That is an example of a nebulous commitment. A better response would be, "I'll get back to you by 5:00pm tomorrow." Clear commitments set reliable expectations for all parties involved. This ensures that you know you are keeping your commitments, and that others know this as well.

3. Identify commitments you are already keeping

Out of habit, you already keep commitments every day. Those actions became habits because you kept your commitment to yourself at some point. Acknowledge those commitments, and give yourself the credit you deserve.

4. Stop making commitments you cannot keep

Once you become aware of the commitments you are making to yourself and to others, stop making commitments you know you cannot keep. It is better to tell your partners that you cannot get something done by a certain deadline than to tell them you can. This is also true as it relates to your family, your friends, your staff, and your patients.

5. Let people know the moment you realize you can no longer keep a commitment you have made

Times will inevitably arise when you cannot keep a commitment you have previously made. When this happens, the best thing you can do is let the other party know as soon as possible. If you know you will be late, tell someone as soon as you know. For example, ask the receptionist to let everyone who has checked in know that you are currently running 20 minutes behind. People are more forgiving when they know ahead of time that their expectations cannot be met.

6. Take inventory of your "commitment keeping" on a regular basis

Commitment keeping is a lifelong journey. It is important to check in with yourself on a regular basis. Even though it begins in your personal life, we share this as the first issue in this chapter on practice management. Without integrity–consistently and dependably delivering on your commitments–nothing else we discuss will matter as it relates to the long-term health of your practice.

> **The bottom line: There is little your practice can do to survive if it does not maintain a long-term reputation for integrity.**

Long-Term Vision

Integrity by itself is not enough. Another key problem that practices face is that they fail to give enough attention to the long-term future of the practice. A great practice manager, who does it right, shared the following:

> *In every decision we make as a practice, our doctors are thinking about the next fifteen to twenty years, and what impact a decision today will make on that time period.* [76]

Without a long-term thought pattern, practices get blown about by the wind, and are distracted by everything that smells like an opportunity. It is surprising to us how rarely medical practices have a guiding mission statement or strategic vision that they can reference. In an IBM report completed after the economic meltdown in 2008, the company sought to identify the characteristics of companies that bounced back the quickest from economic downturn. The report concludes that these select companies "demonstrate the power of having a strategic vision that can thrive in even the toughest of times." If the leadership of your practice does not know where your ship is headed, how can you ever impart this knowledge to your crew? [77]

Transferring the Vision

Once a long-term vision exists, it needs to be communicated across the entire organization. How can you accomplish this? Leadership expert and author, John Maxwell, suggests the following:

1. State your mission and vision in a way that people can understand by communicating with them at their level.
2. Make sure the mission statement and strategic plan are constantly in front of everyone in the organization. [78]

People want something great for which to strive. If you have a mission statement or a defining vision clarifying the direction your organization is headed, could your practice's receptionist clearly articulate it? If not, do not expect it to be carried out at that level of your practice.

> *As with any great team, all team members know the goals and their roles in carrying them out.*
> – Stephen Covey [79]

The Right People

Once the vision has been established and communicated effectively, it is essential to have the right people at your practice. This requires more than a competent, fast-moving physician or PA. Rather, for a healthy practice, the right mix of people is required.

A great practice leader is not looking to bring in the doctor with the highest IQ or fastest hands. Instead, the leader wants someone who can mesh well with the rest of the group–who has some personality, and will come out of the O/R making the group look good.

Reputation is absolutely essential when it comes to building a thriving practice, and nothing can help or hinder your reputation more than the people you hire. For this reason, we ask groups to remember that *every single* person they hire–whether a physician, a receptionist, a coder, an NP, etc.–will have a direct impact on their reputation. The question everyone ought to be asking before they make a final hiring decision is, "Will this person help or hurt our reputation?" There is no middle ground on this issue. Every employee and physician in the group does one or the other.

Leonard Berry and Kent Seltman concur with this assessment in their book, *Management Lessons from the Mayo Clinic*. They submit the following:

> *...organizational excellence is never only about the science. It also is about the 'artistry'...the human touch, teaching, collaboration, generous acts, personal courage, and core values that guide decision making and inspire extra effort* [80]

When it comes to hiring the right people, the other key is to fire the wrong people. If someone is the wrong fit for the practice, remove that person as fast as you can. Before firing, though, realize that often the problem is not with the person, but rather with the process. Most people genuinely want to do the right thing for your practice. Most employees and physicians take pride in the work that they do. Far too often, a bad process is mistaken for a bad person, and that can cause a big problem for the bottom line.

> **It has been said that we judge everyone else by his or her actions, but only judge ourselves based on our intent.**

When it comes to job performance and considering whether or not to "remove someone," we suggest you ask these specific questions in the following order:

1. Is a problem in our process causing our issues with this employee?
2. Is a lack of training causing our issues with this employee?
3. Does this employee genuinely want to do things right?
4. Does this employee have the capability to do things right if #1 and/or #2 are solved?
5. Is this employee holding others back from achieving stronger performance?
6. Is this employee hurting our reputation in a way that cannot be fixed by #1 or #2 above?

Problems with processes and training are prevalent in the business world, and the medical field is no exception. The Mayo Clinic's policy of "teach, don't blame" is missing from many practices.[80] Errors and mistakes represent some of the best teaching opportunities your practice will ever have. It is a blessing if an employee makes a $500 mistake. As long as he learns from it, this could prevent him from making a $50,000 mistake down the road.

If the process is the problem, you are better off keeping your employee and fixing the process. Result: You get the best of both worlds. If training is the problem, help the employee get more training. Better yet, have them document the process while they receive the training so that it is much easier to teach the next person coming through the system to better learn the process.

In our experience, the questions above lead to the four reasons it makes sense to let an employee go:[68]

---

[68] Labor laws vary greatly on a state-by-state basis. Check with your labor and employment attorney to make sure they have no legal concerns prior to implementing these guidelines in your practice.

Reasons to Fire an Employee

1. The employee has no desire to do the right thing. Some people just do not care, and these people need to go. You can see this when a standard has been clearly communicated, and the employee has received sufficient training, yet the expected outcome is still not met through conscious disregard for the standard.

2. The employee has no capacity to complete required tasks. You might have the nicest person in town, but if she does not have the ability to meet stated job requirements, she needs to be removed unless additional training can resolve the issue. You are hurting both the practice and the employee if you keep her in a position she is incapable of fulfilling. Let her go or move her to a position where she has the capacity to succeed.

3. The employee is keeping others from reaching their potential. These employees are the cancer cells of the workplace. They move from cube to cube, or room to room, leaving destruction in their path. More often than not, this destruction is spread through gossip, meddling, or short tempers. Even if these employees are great at their own job, if they are cancer to others, they need to go.

4. Finally, have a zero tolerance policy for employees who are hurting your practice's reputation through blatant disregard for your policies. There is no room for this when your reputation means everything to the future financial health of your practice. Let us clarify--employee mistakes should rarely hurt your reputation. Mistakes should be expected. Patients and consumers want to see your response when mistakes occur. Provided your response is fair and quick, a mistake can often do much to enhance your reputation with others. Mistakes are not a cause for firing someone in most instances. Rather, responses to to mistakes are what will make or break your practice's reputation.

Putting People in the Right Roles

It is not enough just to have well-meaning, talented people at the practice. You also need those well-meaning people sitting in the right positions/jobs/roles. In the great business classic, *Good to Great*, Jim Collins suggests executives who transformed their organizations from good to great, did so with the following attitude:

If we get the right people on the bus, the right people in the right seats, and the wrong people off the bus, then we'll figure out how to take it someplace great. [81]

Too often we see physicians asking the right person to do the wrong thing. We encourage medical groups to put potential employees through testing in advance of hiring to better understand how the employee is wired. Large corporations routinely complete such testing, but we find that many mid-size practices neglect it at great expense to their bottom line. Employees make the best decisions when allowed to trust and act on their instincts. By doing some strategic testing up front, job candidates who are not a good fit can be weeded out much earlier in the process. [82]

For access to further information on employee testing, visit
www.LarsonFinancial.com/EmployeeTesting

Recent Example

Through one testing method we appreciate, the Kolbe Inventory, employees are graded on their energy threshold in four distinct areas: Fact Finding, Follow Through, Quick Starting, and Implementing. The inventory allows managers (perhaps this is you) to quickly understand what is reasonable to expect from a potential employee, and what is not. For example, we would expect anyone involved in coding or collections to have a strong battery for Fact Finding and Follow Through. Physicians should have a high Implementation battery (hands on), or they will burn out too quickly on the job. Practice managers should have a high Quick Start and Fact Finding battery, or they will not be able to manage their job because they have too many bosses to handle all at once.

The point is that different people are geared for different types of work, and it would be a mistake to assign a role to a person for which he has a very low energy threshold. It is not just the role, but also the type of duties within that role that matter.

In addition to the four aspects of the Kolbe Inventory, we ask our physicians and practice managers to look at their employees through the lenses of *Entrepreneur, Manager,* and *Technician* as described by Michael Gerber in his book, *The E-Myth Physician.* Every strong enterprise must operate with all three levels working in tandem with one another. Gerber suggests that people are hard wired to a primary mode of operation. If you are looking for someone to come in and maintain a process, you need a technician. Do not hire someone for this role who is hard wired to be an entrepreneur, because all they will want to do is reinvent and change the process. Vice versa, if you want someone to manage a process for the implementation of a new service you will be providing, do not ask a technician to do this job, or everyone will face disappointment. [75]

Once you have good processes and training in place, the right people on the bus in the right seats, performing the right duties, the next key to a thriving practice is constant communication.

Communication

An un-communicated expectation is usually little more than a disappointment waiting to happen. Often when leaders of a practice are disappointed, they have an expectation in their minds, but have never clearly communicated it to anyone else.

- If you find yourself disappointed by an outcome or an action, trace your steps backward.
- Ask if your expectation was ever truly made clear.
- Check if it may have been more vaguely communicated than you realized.
- If the expectation was never made clear, and it usually was not, you have no one to be disappointed with but yourself.
- When in doubt, *over* clarify.
- It is a good practice to make sure someone can repeat the expectations back to you or has at least confirmed receipt.

The physicians who have the best team of people surrounding them are those that clearly communicate their expectations on a continual basis.

> **Remember, people are for the most part impossible to manage. The key is to manage the system, not the people.**

This is where constant communication comes into play, especially when working through the interpersonal issues that inevitably arise.

Information vs. Empathy
Much interpersonal frustration occurs when the lines between information and empathy get crossed. Often, someone wants information, but only receives empathy, or someone wants empathy, but only receives information. This happens between spouses and colleagues every day. [83]

The difference between information and empathy:
Husband says, "Hi honey, how was your day?"

"Oh, you'll never believe the day I had. I scratched the car, and the kids have been nagging on me, and I'm still nervous about Betsy's piano recital."

Husband responds, "Well, next time maybe it would help if you park a little farther out. Just tell the kids to leave you alone, and tell Betsy to practice more."

How well do you think that conversation turned out? The spouse was simply looking for empathy for a tough day, and instead received information. This is just as important with employees and other interpersonal relationships within the office. Be sure to differentiate if your colleague or employee is seeking information or empathy. This skill greatly enhances relationships and ongoing communication.

Use Problem-Solving Language
Very little gets solved when people lose sight of the problem at hand, which is often the case in the workplace. At the root of this issue is the misuse of language. Oftentimes language is used that causes a defensive

reaction instead of a problem-solving one. Consider the following examples:

- *"Why do you always enter the billable amount the wrong way, Tim?"*
- *"You're not doing what I asked you to do!"*

Both of these statements are unlikely to solve any problems, and instead, are likely to worsen them. Consider the following four principles to make inter-office communication more productive:

1. **Avoid using the word "you" whenever possible, unless in positive conversation.** Even when referring to ourselves in harmless stories, we often use the word "you" in a generalized way. This is an easy way to make someone feel defensive for no reason.

Recent Example

"Wow, anytime you go to that restaurant they always ignore you there."

What this person is actually saying is, "Wow, anytime I go to that restaurant they always ignore me there." Often it is with harmless intent, but the use of "you" creates too many opportunities for someone to take things personally.

To solve this, when telling a personal story, try to use the words "I," "my," etc. Consider the example above, "Every time I go to that restaurant they always ignore me." Now the listener cannot mistake your general statement as a personal attack or judgment.

2. **Avoid the use of absolute words.** Using the words "always" and "never" often create a defensive atmosphere. "You *always* mess up the patient reports." The hearer loses sight of the larger problem, and is now defensive because he or she doesn't always mess up the reports; it is only 95% of the time. In *Crucial Conversations*, Patterson, et al. consider the use of absolutes as a method of violence within communication. Removing this distraction will help to make your message more clear. [84]

3. **If a problem exists, ask for help.** People want to help correct problems, not be blamed for them. If they are the cause, they will often understand this when the problem is put in front of them, rather than you telling them it is their fault.

4. **Soft words turn away anger.** Words such as "perhaps" and "share with me" are very soft, and can be a great introduction to a tough topic in a way that gets the dialogue flowing.

Now let's take our original statements from above and rephrase them with these four principles in mind:

Original
"Why do you always enter the billable amount the wrong way, Tim?"

Improved
"Tim, share with me how you think we can best correct the breakdown in the billing reports?"

Original
"You're not doing what I asked you to do!"

Improved
"Hi Jenny. May I please share something I noticed during that last procedure? I realized that perhaps I haven't done the best job of communicating my full expectations, and it seems you have the desire to do a great job. My expectation is that... Do you think you can help make sure that happens moving forward?"

You can change the language in each of these examples many ways to make them more productive for you, but the examples above show wording that gets to the heart of the problem, and keeps everyone focused on solving it.

Beware Email and Text Etiquette and Accidental Tone
Email and text messaging are fast becoming our preferred communication methods as a society. Though the information exchange is great, we have not yet established strong standards of etiquette for

digital communication, which means effective communication through these forms can be challenging.

Consider the following to generate more successful electronic communication:

- Avoid using ALL CAPS as it might accidentally make people feel like you are yelling at them.
- Begin emails with a salutation–even if your email is a quick response to someone else. When someone starts out by reading "Hello Jim" or "Hi Rose," it warms up whatever may follow.
- When in doubt, tell the tone you are writing with. When we speak face to face, we can understand intent much easier than we can through written word. Nothing is wrong with saying "Please note that I'm writing this note with _____ in mind: (fill in the blank with "great appreciation," "a heavy heart," "a smile on my face," etc.). Avoid confusion by not allowing room for confusion.

Have Their Backs

People will move mountains for you if they know unquestionably that you support them unconditionally. Three suggestions for making sure your team knows that you have their backs:

1. The best way to establish a supportive atmosphere is to have a strong policy against gossiping or complaining about someone else who is not around.

Recent Example

One physician had a big problem with gossip in his office. He made it very clear to his employees that if they had a legitimate complaint about a co-worker, they had to be willing to share it face-to-face with that person. The next time someone came to his office to complain, he asked her to hold on for a moment. Next he picked up the phone and asked the second person to come to his office. "Please proceed," he told the first employee.

This policy establishes a team atmosphere where differences will be worked out in a straightforward way. It also says: I have all of your backs. It is shocking how fast the gossip and complaining stops when people understand that they will no longer have the opportunity to talk about someone else behind his or her back.

2. Actually have their backs when a problem comes up. People typically want to do the right thing, so when wrong things happen, this indicates a breakdown in the process. System breakdowns are our fault as leaders. Too often we find ourselves quick to shift the blame in order to make ourselves look better, when in reality, we look best when we make our people look best. Very little goes on in the day-to-day realm of your practice for which you or your leadership team is not ultimately responsible. When a problem arises—and it will soon—the best response you can have is to take responsibility. Use it as a teaching moment with the accidental offender. A personal mentor used to always say that if you have a problem, build a process, and you will no longer have a problem.[69]

3. Finally, when it comes to supporting your staff, keep your "teaching moments" (a positive spin on "reprimands") private. Limit the interaction to only those who need to be a part of it. In other words, calling someone out about a problem in a group setting is usually a bad idea, but never addressing the issue is also a mistake. Set aside some time when everyone is removed from the direct situation to discuss the issue, and seek to find a solution that will prevent it from reoccurring. Do not use email to reprimand. Face-to-face interaction is the best way to ensure your message is received the way it is intended, and it helps re-enforce a strong relationship with the employee.

Strategic and Tactical Time

In a medical world that is crying out for you as a doctor to "See more patients!" the following discussion could not be more relevant. As a physician who also wears a hat as a business owner or practice leader, your time can be divided into two distinct categories: Strategic and Tactical.

---

[69] Rick Phillips, President of Phillips Financial Services, Inc. (who gives credit to his friend and mentor John Behrendt for teaching this to him).

Tactical time is spent working on patient care, procedures, pre-op, post-op, office visits, etc. Today nearly 100% of residency and fellowship training is focused on this time as a *technician.* Think of tactical time as any time you are wearing your "physician" hat.

Strategic time belongs to wearing your "business owner" or *entrepreneur* hat. This is time spent thinking through the long-term direction of your practice, furthering your education, bettering your business, or bettering yourself. Physicians receive little to no training on this during residency. However, this will ultimately make or break a private practice.

Think of it this way. Often the general on the battlefield is one of the best sharpshooters in the bunch. He has had years of training and experience, and can do a great job on the front lines. But is this the *best* use of his time? No way! This leader's time is best spent drawing up the battle plan and looking at the big picture. Unfortunately, many physicians think their time is too valuable to spend in the war room, working *on* the business instead of *in* the business. Direct result: Most practices are dysfunctional.

When it comes to building a strategic focus into your practice, a doctor has two viable options:

1. Carve out time to spend together as the leaders of the practice discussing strategy. This is when you put on your *entrepreneur* hats. Up front, spend a minimum of at least half a day per week to work on taking the practice closer to its fullest potential.

2. Or, hire a solid leader to serve as your practice manager. Get out of his way so that he can spend this strategic entrepreneur time on your behalf. A practice manager who can lead your practice against the backdrop of your long-term vision is worth many times more than you thought you were willing to pay. Unfortunately, many groups are pennywise and pound foolish about this aspect of their practice–and their bottom line suffers as a result.

Those are your only options. This is tough for many physicians to swallow. As medical management expert, Michel Gerber, says,

Because most Doctors are control freaks, 99% of today's medical companies are practices, not businesses.[75]

Profit Maximization

Let's face the brutal fact: The business side of medicine is becoming increasingly complex. "Seeing more patients" no longer works. Though inflation continues to rise, Medicare reimbursements continue to decrease. Eventually every physician hits a point where "seeing more patients" is impossible, while trying to maintain any kind of family or social life.

What is the new solution? We believe it rests with medical practices learning to run more like franchises rather than charities or government institutions. To do this, the practice should begin by building an actual business plan. Most practices have not strategically looked at their business plan in years, if they even have one. Without a roadmap to where they are headed, the practice becomes dysfunctional. Why? Each partner might have different visions for the practice's priorities.

Take for example a surgical specialty practice we encountered in Texas. They recently lost a partner because he was convinced that a particular ancillary service was the way of the future. When the other partners did not share his vision, he left so that he could build his vision somewhere else. From our perspective, it appeared the bigger problem was that the practice did not have an overall vision, so their only defense was to tell the partner how bad his idea was. Instead, they should have been able to quickly refer to their business plan and show the partner how his ideas were not in line with what they wanted for the future.

It is time to dust off the business plan or begin anew. These items need to be covered:

Components of a Successful Medical Business Plan
Revenue Drivers
- Marketing plan
- Key contracts
- Ancillaries
- Services provided
- Coding efficiencies
- Potential revenue drivers

Expense Drivers
- Physician compensation plan
- Corporate structure

- Key expenses
- Wasted physician time
- Competition
- Workflow and processes
- Benefits

Results
- Benchmarking progress

We know it can be overwhelming for a physician to think about these things, but this is your solution to maximizing profit without having to "see more patients." If you do not take the time, no one else is likely to either. Be the catalyst that drives the practice to spend the time on these things.

The following are some conversation starters for each of these topics to get your creative juices flowing, and keep you all on point:

The Marketing Plan
To maximize the efficiency of your marketing plan, it helps to start with a list itemizing where your marketing dollars are currently being spent. The practice or marketing department should be able to provide this list fairly easily. As you examine the list, which of these items do you know to be highly effective? This is often difficult to answer because operations have been "business as usual" for a long time. This indicates the need for better communication with patients. You want to know what is bringing them to your door. A marketing firm can help you develop a communication process to better understand why your patients are choosing your practice.

It shocks many practices, but most patients usually come in the door from two major sources, 1) referrals from a particular complementary group, or 2) your group is well-known for a particular procedure/specialty. This is good news. Once your practice has identified its major door openers, you can stop investing in the other methods that are not producing consistent results. Then, put at least half of what was being spent elsewhere toward further developing the most effective methods. The compounded results are amazing.

Note: *It is unwise to expect referrals to be the main driver of patient volume with no effort on your practice's part. Instead, a successful practice will actively explore marketing opportunities to increase new patient volume to its desired levels, and will continually seek to further develop its existing referral relationships, instead of taking them for granted.*

Key Contracts

Too many groups pay too little attention to their key contracts. If your group is connected with a hospital, do not take this for granted, even if you are the only "game" in town. Dedicate resources to ensure your relationship with the hospital remains strong. Contract negotiations should be a gradual process as the old contract is winding down. If renewing a contract requires a full-out negotiation process, proper communication was lacking along the way. Rarely should there be any surprises during negotiation when it comes to key contracts your group has established. By staying in constant communication, you should be able to sense any major changes long before the old contract expires. Someone on the team must have the direct responsibility for this function though.

Additionally, other key contracts with your main insurance payors should be under constant review and aggressively negotiated on a regular basis. We have seen physicians who were able to significantly increase their compensation simply by negotiating for better reimbursements from insurance companies. If you are not regularly pushing on this, or benefiting from economies of scale, someone needs to give it more attention.

Ancillaries

What ancillary services don't you provide that you should? These can create great passive income streams to help augment procedural income.

- What are other physicians in your specialty offering in terms of ancillary services?
- How has it impacted their bottom line?
- What can you learn from them as you implement these services for your own practice?
- What business are you consistently referring out the door?
- Is there a way to keep this lost revenue in-house?

Services Offered

What services generate the most revenue for your practice? Are these the services that you enjoy providing? We have encountered several practices that offer procedures the physicians do not enjoy because they think these procedures lead them to the opportunities they do enjoy. That is often not the case. Most physicians need a "stop-doing list," a list of all of the things that are wasting more time or energy than they are worth.

- What services do you need to stop offering?
- What services do you need to start offering?

Coding Efficiencies

We could have easily included coding *inefficiencies* as an expense driver. For most practices, though, making their coding more efficient is a big opportunity for a revenue increase.

Recent Example

One of the billing and coding specialists we work with tracks the average extra collections increase they are able to generate for a client. To date, they have consistently increased collections for practices by a minimum of 8% per year. For a practice that is used to collecting $10 million, this is an $800,000 increase in revenue, with no extra patients seen.

For a twelve-physician group, this would generate an additional $67,000 in revenue per year per physician. That is serious money being left on the table.

Hiring out your coding is the general "best practice" we have encountered when it comes to billing. It rarely makes sense to try to do it in-house because too many mistakes are made. Some of the worst coders we have encountered are large university or hospital systems. Physicians tell us horror stories of procedures that never get billed.

Note: *For a doctor working in a large institutional setting, we would be hesitant to recommend accepting a contract based on collections* *unless you have some direct input into the coding and billing process at the institution. We would expect you to have access to monthly reports at a minimum, so that you can keep your finger on the pulse of the billing process management.*

To put it bluntly, if you are paying for in-house staff to do your billing and collecting, you are probably wasting money. Our experience is that an outside company that properly educates your team will more than pay for itself in the work it does for your group, and will have economies of scale and leverage from which your practice can benefit.

Potential Revenue Drivers
- What other revenue streams are you missing?
- Are there collaborative opportunities you should be exploring that could minimize your competition in town?
- Is there a surgery-center opportunity that you need to further investigate?

The Physician Compensation Plan
Physician compensation can be one of the toughest areas for a group to address. A lot of intangibles can make it tough to put a fair value on work provided by each individual physician in the group. Some practices handle this by being purely socialistic in nature, delivering equal compensation regardless of number of procedures done/patients seen, while others handle it by employing a completely "eat what you kill" model. Expenses further complicate the issue. For example, if using the "eat what you kill" model, who gets charged for what expenses? We do not have absolute answers because this is a group-specific issue. However, these are some general principles that can help guide the discussion:

- How did the current compensation-sharing structure come into existence? Does this have any bearing on what should be in place today?
- How fair does it seem to the group currently? Keep in mind you could be opening up Pandora's Box here, so do not ask this question unless you really want honest input. Also, realize that it is very rare for everyone in the group to feel fairly compensated. There is seldom, if ever, a perfect solution that will make everyone 100% happy, so agree

up front that the goal is not to make everyone happy, but instead to arrive at the solution that best benefits the future of the group for the next ten to twenty years.

- What options does the group have for bettering the compensation structure moving forward in order to make the practice stronger over the next decade or two?

Corporate Structure

Many groups are still operating the same way because it is what they have always done. Depending on the state where your practice is located, practice structure can have a profound impact on the income that makes its way directly into your pocket. While no cookie cutter answer is given here, a couple of main planning opportunities may exist that your group has not yet explored.

Are your real estate and equipment owned by entities separate from the medical practice? If so, you can pay a reasonable market rent to these entities as this could help to eliminate unnecessary social security and Medicare taxes for your physicians.

Have you explored the option of having your physicians act as independent contractors within the group structure? This, too, can offer tremendous tax saving opportunities to your physicians.

Recent Example

One large multi-specialty clinic we work with has all partners establish their own Professional Corporation (PC). The physician's PC contracts for services with the clinic. The physicians still share employee benefits, but it gives them the opportunity to take control of their own business deductions and supplemental employee benefit plans, as well as puts the decision of how much to treat as wages vs. distributions on each doctor's own shoulders.

Key Expenses

Aside from physician compensation, can you name your practice's top three expenses? Most physicians cannot. How can you control these expenses if you are not aware of what they are? When was the last time you went through your expenses as a group to determine items that were unnecessary? Again, there will always be some disagreement here, so determine up front what the ground rules will be for making a decision.

Wasted Physician Time

We would suggest that wasted physician time is usually one of the key phantom expenses that will not show up on your financial statements. This happens when medical care does not get handed down to the lowest cost provider of that care. Obviously a balance must be maintained here, but most industries have learned about going "lean" and "defect free." Part of being "lean" as a medical group is not allowing your physicians to do things lower-cost employees can do just as well. A specialized physician's time spent practicing his or her specialty is worth $500–$2,000+ per hour, so realize that it is actually irresponsible for you as a physician to waste your time 1) doing anything besides seeing and treating patients in the procedures that only you as a physician can do, or 2) taking strategic time to work on areas of your practice. Lower-cost providers should handle everything else.

Competition

When was the last time your group performed a SWOT analysis on your greatest competitors? A SWOT analysis seeks to understand their Strengths, Weaknesses, Opportunities, and Threats. It would also be helpful to know what kind of SWOT analysis they might complete on you. The good news is that they probably are not spending time thinking strategically about these issues, so you will already have an advantage on the competition.

Workflow and Processes

Does your practice have documented procedures and systems in place? Here is the best test you can give your practice: How long would it take someone new in each staff position to learn the systems? How would they learn them?

The reality is that rarely are processes in place, let alone documented processes and a systematic training system. As a result, groups spend hundreds of thousands of dollars in wasted money. Why? Because everyone learns to do something his or her own way, and every change to the process creates an additional expense of resources to the group.

Ask yourselves: What would it take for us to be able to franchise our practice to someone else? Franchise creators are some of our favorite entrepreneurs. They understand the value in building strong systems–so strong that they go out and sell the systems, instead of the actual products that they manufacture or the services they provide. Management consultant, Michael Gerber, shares emphatically:

> *The value of your equity is directly proportional to how well your practice works. And how well your practice works is directly proportional to the effectiveness of the systems you have put into place...*[75]

We are not necessarily suggesting you should go franchise your practice, but maybe this is another potential revenue driver you should be seeking. Dentists have done this for decades and have made fortunes doing so.

Here are the steps to getting successful systems in place that will save your practice time and money:

1. Identify the best practice for each process that occurs regularly in your office.
2. Document the process. Note: do not try to fix them all yet, that will come later.
3. Once the process is documented, look for ways to improve the process. Usually the person doing the job is the one most qualified to answer this question. This gives him or her a chance to feel valuable as well, because you are genuinely seeking input.
4. If there is a better way to do the process, get the updated method documented.
5. Although it may be a cultural shift, ask people to start following the protocol. However, let them know you value their input, and if they see a better way to do something, they should let their manager know.
6. Once the processes are in good shape and well documented, the next key task becomes making the processes easy to teach/train/learn.
7. Once people are trained in the processes, it is the manager's job to manage the processes.

As it relates to the training step in the process, one of the best training systems we have ever seen comes from an orthopedic device manufacturer. The company handed over their training to their marketing department. It was a brilliant strategy because training is all about finding the easiest way to communicate a concept to an audience. Who better to handle this than the marketing team? On a shoestring budget, the company's marketing team came up with the idea to make brief audio, video, or written segments on each process their employees needed to know or understand. Next they put this collected wisdom into an iPad™ application. The training was:

- **Systematic**–Everyone sees, hears, and/or reads the same thing.
- **Time Minimal**–Technology does the heavy lifting, not other employees who have more important roles to fill.
- **Easy to Update**–Once a process changes, they simply update the data on their central server, and it is immediately updated for everyone across the company.

Results: Benchmarking Progress

Having a plan in place is not enough. Progress needs to be measurable. Once the plan is built, you should be able to easily answer some critical questions:

- What is your revenue expectation for the next quarter? (Now you can track your actual progress against the expected results.)
- What specific action items need to be implemented?
- When will you revisit these to analyze the results?

While first getting started, we suggest you block out time on a quarterly basis. The leadership team should get away from the office to go through the plan to benchmark your results. This is where you can continue to raise the tough questions.

You will recognize that you are on the right track when the following are in place:

1. You know what your expected results are, and they show an increase over previous results.
2. You have a measurable way to track these results to make sure things are moving according to plan.
3. The office is becoming more systematized–even the way the physicians do procedures should be systematized.

4. You have a solid training system in place for every position in your practice.

5. You are in the process of adding a new revenue stream.

This is just a sampling of the benefits you should expect with a well-executed plan in place.

To close out this discussion on practice management, the next chapter will now direct its focus on conveying the important issues related to employee benefits provided by a practice.

PRACTICAL APPLICATION

Your group's reputation means everything. Reputation begins in the collective personal life of the physicians who represent the brand of your practice. A personal lack of integrity on behalf of those in your practice can lead to a very public revenue problem. To thwart this concern, work on developing a culture of commitment keeping.

Seeing more patients is not a viable option for maintaining the same income you have previously enjoyed. Instead, today's medical environment demands that you learn to lead a business, instead of run a practice. To do this, rock-solid mission, vision, and business plans must be instituted before you can move to a more effective business model.

As it relates to your business plan conversations, many groups establish great ideas and intentions, but fail to implement the changes necessary to spur the practice forward. Progress requires *tangible action items* to make something happen. An action item must:

- Be something that can be checked off, and not be nebulous. "Improve the billing system" is not an action item. "Interview three coding specialists" is an action item.
- Have a deadline. Without a deadline, everything can get pushed back.
- Have one person who understands his or her role as the responsible party for the specific action item.

Everyone should know the action items that have been set, and be accountable to the practice for fulfilling his or her commitments. If your practice does not have time to build and implement a sound business plan, you need to hire someone else–a practice manager or consultant–to build and implement a plan for you.

Ignoring these issues, and hoping for the golden years of medicine to return, is a losing proposition. This changing economic environment has presented your practice with an opportunity to grow into an enterprise, and this opportunity should not be wasted.

Note: *Although contracts were lightly discussed in this chapter, this is currently one of the fast evolving topics for physicians. By registering at our web site www.LarsonFinancials.com/Contracts, you will gain access to our free bonus chapter on contract negotiations.*

For further reading:
- *The E-Myth Physician,* by Michael Gerber
- *Good to Great,* by Jim Collins
- *Be a People Person,* by John Maxwell
- *Crucial Conversations,* by Patterson, et al
- *Messages: The Communication Skills Book,* by Matthew McKay
- *Management Lessons from the Mayo Clinic,* by Berry and Seltman

CHAPTER 10

Employee Benefit Plans
Build an Efficient Benefits Structure

"Do Starbuck's employees take coffee breaks?"
-Random blog thought

Benefits and Employee Compensation
(From an Employer Perspective)
Last week we visited with the executive and human resource teams from two large hospital systems and a large multi-specialty clinic. All three organizations have a complex structure of employee benefits in place. Although their specific challenges and opportunities were unique, the challenges they face are common to medical practices and institutions.

Common Employee Benefit Challenges:
1. Competing agendas work against each other from multiple sources:
   a. The Highly Profitable Physicians
   b. The Research Minded Physicians
   c. The Non-Profitable Physicians
   d. The Executive Team
   e. The Finance Department
   f. The HR Department
   g. All Other Employees
2. Rarely do each of these entities have a clear understanding of what the other entity values or is trying to accomplish. Furthermore, many times, they actually think they do understand each other.

3. The benefits already in place are not structured as cost effectively as they should be due to:
   a. Not understanding the relationship of the brokers and vendors from a total compensation standpoint
   b. Not leveraging the economies of scale given to certain brokers that are not provided to other brokers
   c. Utilizing a flawed RFP process when soliciting vendors
   d. Not holistically coordinating the benefits through a harmonized process
   e. Relying on personal relationships of the decision makers rather than seeking the best solution for the enterprise
4. The benefits were not properly established to accomplish the objectives they were designed to achieve.

Recent Example

While visiting with one large hospital system, we learned they were providing a 457(f) plan to their physicians, where the employee can elect to defer compensation into the future, instead of taking it currently. The hospital had a large flaw in the design of the plan though. They required a ten-year commitment from the physicians prior to the money becoming vested. In other words, if a physician left the practice prior to the ten-year marker, he would lose any compensation he had deferred into the future. When we outlined this issue as well as the problems with deferring income into a future, unknown tax rate (possibly greater than today's), it was clear that most physicians should not participate in the plan. The hospital's goal is to keep physicians engaged with the practice long term, but the benefits in place were not meeting the outcome for which they were designed.

At a different hospital system, the Chief Medical Officer said that the top priority of the organization was to retain their most profitable physicians. They sought our input on how to put a benefits structure together that would help retain their best and brightest doctors. Down the hall, the HR department had a totally different agenda. Their goal was to eliminate any benefits that created an idea that some employees were more highly valued than others. In this instance the executive leadership had not done a good job of casting a clear vision for the direction the hospital system needed to be moving in (see page 168).

Employee benefits can be a large expense for a practice or institution, but they do not always have to be. A practice that can train and maintain solid employees is one that shows good signs of strong health. Benefits and compensation are important to keeping the right people, but not as important as many practices believe. Studies have often concluded that people stay with an employer because they like the people they work with, feel appreciated for the work that they do, and have the opportunity to grow and experience new challenges. Compensation and benefits actually rank among the middle group of reasons why employees stay with an employer.[85]

In other words, people want to work with their friends. As an employer, one of the most important things your practice or institution can do is create opportunities for employees to bond outside of the normal work environment. It is in these moments away from the daily grind that people have the opportunity to grow closer to one another. This creates loyalty, and retaining loyal staff can save your practice a lot of money over the years.

Although benefits are not the most important thing when it comes to keeping good people, it is certainly important that your practice does its best to provide high-quality benefits at a reasonable cost. Additionally, keep in mind that the owners and pension decision makers are personally liable for the risks of employee retirement programs, so this area should be of particular concern, even if other benefits are not a current area of focus.

The Types of Employee Benefits

The realm of employee benefits relevant to the medical landscape can be segregated into four different types, which will encompass the remainder of this chapter.

1. Group Retirement Plans
2. Core Benefits
3. Voluntary Benefits
4. Executive Benefits & Golden Handcuffs

Group Retirement Plans

Retirement plans are the most problematic area we encounter for many medical practices, and that is why they receive the most attention in this book. Almost every group mistakenly believes they have a great plan in place, but in reality, most do not even know the right questions to ask to determine whether they have a great plan, or not. We say this with compassion because it is understandably a complicated subject.

Medical groups implement several retirement account options for employees including:

403(b) plans	SEP IRAs
401(k) plans	Simple IRAs
Roth 403(b) plans	Profit Sharing plans
Roth 401(k) plans	Defined Benefit plans
401(a) plans	Cash Balance plans
457(b) plans	Keogh plans
457(f) plans	412(i) plans

> **Visit the following website to learn more about many of the plans above:**
> www.retirementplans.irs.gov/plan-comparison-table

This book will not spend the time required to explain each of these plans in detail. Rather, the most important factor to understand at this point is that, with the exception of the Roth 401(k) and Roth 403(b) all of these plans are taxed as ordinary income when you take funds out to spend and enjoy throughout retirement. By nature, this means that all plans above—Roth plans excluded—will compound your taxes to an unknown future tax rate (see page 70 for a thorough discussion on this issue). Our point is that pre-tax accounts are not as valuable as many physicians and employees believe them to be. As a result, our hope is that physicians and pension committees will begin to take a closer look at the underlying fundamentals of their plans and spend less time analyzing if there is opportunity to defer additional taxes into the future.

Pre-tax accounts are not as valuable as many physicians and employees believe them to be.

Many hospital administrators understand the liability placed on the investment decision makers, but few medical groups do. Through audits of medical group pension plans, we often ask several questions to help the group understand the personal liability held by the owners and retirement plan decision makers. The following is a sampling of the questions that we ask through the course of an audit. Before we pose these questions, two observations:

1. It is normal that many groups cannot answer these questions because they have never received proper training in this area.
2. Remember that as an owner of the practice (especially if you serve on the pension committee), you have personal liability for these issues, so it is worth your time to make sure you have a better understanding of the right questions to ask.

From a formatting standpoint, you will see the audit question first, followed by a *wrong* answer often given by a medical practice in the course of an audit. Finally, we will identify a *best practice* answer–one that a well-informed (and well-protected) group should be able to provide.

Q1. What type of risk is there to a practice that provides a retirement plan to its employees?

Common Wrong Answer:
We have insurance for that, or our plan provides us with a certificate that says we do not need to worry about it.

Best Practice Answer:

You have *substantial* risk. The company has liability for the plan, and the owners of the practice, and the plan decision makers and trustees also have *personal* liability for proper oversight of the plan. If you make a retirement plan available for employees, your practice must make sure that the plan complies properly with your fiduciary duty as established by the Department of Labor under ERISA.

The Uniform Prudent Investor Act helps to define many of your standards as a plan trustee. Most importantly, it suggests plan trustees and fiduciaries should provide *prudent* investment options to plan participants. Most medical groups we encounter, including hospital systems, are not properly satisfying their fiduciary duty as it relates to this specific issue. The bottom line is that you could be personally liable if an employee decides to complain. In many physicians' lives, this is one of the most overlooked areas where the need for asset protection exists.

Q2. How can you best minimize this risk?

Common Wrong Answer:

We meet with our advisor on an annual, or more frequent basis, to discuss the investment choices being provided, and how often they are in communication with each participant.

Best Practice Answer:

Make sure that your advisor is serving in a capacity as a fiduciary of the plan. This way he is on the hook as well if the plan is not properly meeting its duty to participants. Even though many advisors claim verbally they are doing so, they rarely share in the fiduciary liability with the plans that they offer.

Your advisor can serve as a fiduciary of the plan in two primary methods, and the expectation of what role he is fulfilling should be clearly defined by the plan document. Through the course of our audits, we find that very few plans have the fiduciary status of their advisor clearly defined. This is most often due to the advisor failing to fulfill either of the following roles:[86]

ERISA 3(21) Fiduciary

An ERISA 3(21) Fiduciary status means you have engaged the advisor to serve as a co-fiduciary to your group. The advisor is responsible for providing prudent investment recommendations, but the ultimate decisions and responsibility still rest with your group.

ERISA 3(38) Fiduciary

An ERISA 3(38) Fiduciary status has a higher level of authority as it relates to your plan. Nominating a 3(38)Fiduciary is the only way for your group to exculpate yourselves from bearing both corporate and personal liability for the investment options offered to employees under the plan. This status means you have given discretionary authority to an investment advisor to select and monitor your plan's investment options. He or she is not just making recommendations, but also making decisions.

> **Nominating a 3(38) Fiduciary is the only way for your group to exculpate yourselves from personal liability for the employees' investment options.**

Most plans are not currently established with a provider willing to accept the responsibility for the oversight of the plan's investment decisions. It amazes us that so many firms, especially banks, are willing to sell you a pension plan, but not willing to take responsibility for the performance of that plan. Make sure that your plan's advisors are serving in a 3(21) or 3(38) Fiduciary capacity.

Q3. How should we determine which fund managers to replace on a year-by-year basis if we are concerned about their performance?

Common Wrong Answer:
We first move an underperforming fund to a "watch list." If the fund continues to underperform, we replace it as an option in the plan.

Best Practice Answer:

You are asking the wrong question. Refer to the "Investment Management" section beginning on page 56. Most plans should consist primarily of index or institutional asset class funds, as these would not need to be replaced. Index-type funds are considered by many professionals to be the "default standard" by which your plan may be measured in the event of an employee lawsuit.[87]

The Prudent Investor Rule requires that those who are responsible for someone else's assets, need to manage them properly. For this reason alone, we are unwilling to serve as a co-fiduciary of a plan that does not offer a strong mix of index or institutional asset class funds to its participants. It is simply not a risk we are willing to take, and we advise our clients to follow the same course of action. Consider the warning of the American Law Institute in response to plans trying to select a mutual fund they think will perform well in the future:[36]

> Fiduciaries and other investors are confronted with potent evidence that the application of expertise, investigation, and diligence in efforts to "beat the market" ordinarily promises little or no payoff, or even a negative payoff after taking account of research and transaction costs...
>
> Evidence shows that there is little correlation between fund managers' earlier successes and their ability to produce above-market returns in subsequent periods.

Although this is the value-add most plan providers promote, trying to select the "hot" funds is a losing proposition. There is little evidence suggesting that anyone can consistently pick the hot funds for a pension plan. Many plans go through an ongoing process of firing fund managers every few quarters, due to underperformance, compared to their benchmarks. These plan participants get access to the "hot" funds after they have already been hot because they get chosen in a rear-view mirror. One recent study looked at the hiring decisions of plan leadership over a six-year period for almost 3,500 different employer-sponsored retirement plans. The study found that the funds chosen to replace old funds had outperformed the old funds substantially in the three years leading up to the change. However, after hiring the new funds, they actually underperformed the old funds in the three years following the

> *The failure to provide investment options that deliver consistent market results is a lawsuit waiting to happen.*

change. In other words, even though index results are still better, the plans would have been better off keeping their underperforming funds rather than selling them off to attempt to deliver over-performing funds.[70]

The failure to provide investment options that deliver consistent market results is a lawsuit waiting to happen. Any retirement plan that provides actively managed funds, as its primary investment options, might have to justify this poor decision in a courtroom at some point. If you find yourself in this position, how will you defend yourself in the face of so much academic evidence that it was a poor decision?

The best practice here is to offer index funds or institutional asset class funds in your plan so that your employees will receive consistent market results.

Recent Example

The younger physicians in a large surgical group have taken the time to understand prudent investment principles, but the older physicians play golf with the current plan advisor. The plan is clearly lacking on meeting its fiduciary duties to employees. There is clear evidence that the older physicians keep firing the existing funds in order to buy "better" funds moving forward.

Every year or two, the underperforming funds get fired, and the older physicians and their golf buddy advisor, select new funds that have performed very well over the past decade to replace these funds. Not surprising, the new funds end up

---

[70] Source: Goyal and Wahal (2008), based on 8,775 hiring decisions by 3,417 plan sponsors delegating $627 billion in assets; and 869 firing decisions by 482 plan sponsors withdrawing $105 billion in assets.

underperforming their market benchmarks. They get moved
to a "watch list" first, and eventually get fired. Several asset
classes are on their fourth or fifth round of funds in the past
decade. The plan often holds the funds that have been hot
performers in the past, but the employees never get the hot
results from these funds going forward. This is what happens
when investments are selected in a rear-view mirror.

This arrangement increases the potential for a lawsuit, and
the younger partners in the group want to fix this, but the
older partners do not want to upset their golf buddy. The irony
is he has zero liability because he is not serving in a fiduciary
capacity for the plan. The advisor has no real skin in the game,
but he is putting the group at great risk.

Q4. How do we best help our employees make their investment decisions within the plan?

Common Wrong Answer:
We give them access to do whatever they want to do.

Best Practice Answer:
Provide them with two resources:
1. Access to professional advice. Many plans do not offer one-on-one professional advice to participants. This is a big mistake. A recent study determined that employee use of professional help and guidance is one of the greatest contributing factors in 401(k) success for participants. [88]
2. A solid mix of predetermined asset allocation models properly constructed by professionals. In other words, the employee works with an advisor to choose an appropriate risk model. The advisor helps to make the investment decisions for the employee in coordination with the employee's chosen level or risk tolerance.

The article, "The Tyranny of Choice" from the *Journal of Pension Benefits*, confirms this approach by acknowledging:

*Instead of forcing participants to make their own investment
decisions, we have to provide a simplified means for participants
to achieve truly effective diversification... a move toward "advisor
managed portfolios" must take place. Such portfolios free
participants from the asset allocation burden while still allowing for
the flexibility of self-direction.* [89]

Employees do not, for the most part, want the flexibility they once
thought they did. Rather, they want help ensuring they make good
decisions with their retirement dollars. By providing employees with
limited investment choices and one-on-one professional advice, the plan
is best equipped for strong results.

Q5. What fees are we paying in our plan?

Common Wrong Answer:
We are not sure of all of the plan expenses.

Best Practice Answer:
In any retirement plan, several different fees are either hidden from
participants, or fully disclosed. You should have a clear understanding
of what you pay for record keeping, investment management,
administrative, and advisor fees. You should also be ahead of the
required schedule in making sure these fees are properly disclosed to
plan participants.

Many plans mistakenly believe they have a "low-cost" plan, but few
actually understand what this means. Plans that have "revenue-sharing"
arrangements believe they are saving money for participants. Often this
is little more than a rebating process where participants are overcharged
to begin with, then a portion of this expense is refunded to them. We
believe the actual expenses of the plan remain relatively large.

A new requirement was recently passed by the Department of
Labor requiring plans to begin fully disclosing fees to all participants
by January 1, 2012. This will be an eye-opening experience for many
employees.[90]

In addition to the basic questions outlined above, we have identified
more than fifty other questions a plan needs to be able to answer in
order to properly satisfy its fiduciary responsibility to its participants.

> **For additional information on these topics, please click the following link to access our Retirement Plan Audit Checklist:**
> *www.LarsonFinancial.com/RetirementPlans*

Core Benefits

In addition to offering retirement plans, core benefits are offered by most medical groups to their employees.

Core benefits primarily consist of the following:
- Group Health Insurance
- Dental Insurance
- Vision Insurance
- Short-term Disability Insurance
- Long-term Disability Insurance
- Group Long-term Care Insurance
- Group Life Insurance

Not all of the above benefits are covered in detail, but it should be noted that we believe it is essential to look at these benefits through a comprehensive filter to ensure that they are operating efficiently with one another. To best fulfill the purposes of this book, we will stick to those issues within core benefits that create the most important opportunities or weaknesses for the physicians we encounter.

Group Health Insurance

Group health insurance helps to spread the risk of employee health care costs. Four main concepts have recently been fundamental to helping employers reduce or levelize their costs in this area:[91]

1. Employee Cost Sharing

It has long been sacred to many medical groups to provide health care free of charge to employees–after all, you're in the healthcare business. "Free healthcare" has disappeared in the workplace in every sector except for healthcare. It's time for healthcare groups to catch up, and start sharing some of this cost with employees. For many of the groups we've worked with, we have suggested they provide a percentage of the actual employees' coverage, and a much smaller percentage of any dependent's coverage. It is amazing how quickly people admit that their spouse already has coverage elsewhere when they have to pay for it through your group.

2. HSA Plans[58]

Health Savings Accounts have gained considerable popularity in recent years. Think of an HSA plan as giving employees a higher deductible, but agreeing that you, as the group, will pay for a portion of the increased deductible. Why do this? Because it often cuts premiums for the cost of the underlying insurance. Provided that more people in the group are healthier than not, this can be a major cost-saving move for the employer that has zero initial out-of-pocket hit to employees. The downside is that switching to this type of plan is educationally intensive because employees need to begin using a new debit card, and they no longer have the familiar small co-pay. These plans also offer some potential investment benefits that can be attractive, if structured properly.

3. HRA Plans[58]

Health Reimbursement Arrangements are perhaps one of the most under-utilized tools for medical groups. HRA plans work by determining the maximum amount of health expenses an employee can have reimbursed by the group, determined annually by the plan. HRAs are best utilized by groups that consist primarily of physicians. In a smaller group setting, the amount of reimbursement provided can simply be deducted from the physician's productivity pool, so that the practice profit is not reduced based on an individual's medical bills. This ultimately results in giving the physician an unlimited bucket with which to pay healthcare costs with pre-tax dollars. This can result in thousands of dollars of cost savings any time a physician has significant ongoing healthcare costs. The reason being that normally these expenses are only deductible above the 7.5% income threshold, and few physicians ever reach this target. Instead, by using the HRA plan described above, these expenses can be paid pre-tax from the first dollar.[71]

---

[71] The size of the group has a lot to do with the proper way to set up a plan like this, and it is essential to work with a knowledgeable tax professional to properly coordinate this benefit into your plan structure.

4. HMO Plans[92]

Health Maintenance Organizations (HMOs) have been criticized in the past due primarily to frustrations over not having open access to providers. However, this landscape has changed, and many insurance carriers have moved to a stronger open-access arrangement. In some states, HMOs are another potential platform a medical group can use to save substantial premium dollars without sacrificing employee convenience.

Group Disability Insurance

We find that seven out of ten physicians do not have their disability insurance structured properly because not all specialty-specific coverage is created equally. (See a more thorough explanation of this issue on page 45-46.)

When it comes to your practice, you need to understand these four important aspects:

1. Group disability coverage is changeable by the insurance company, whereas individual coverage is not. In other words, group contracts allow the insurance company to change the terms of the coverage, instead of locking them in. This is a difference that cannot be ignored.
2. Group disability coverage is rarely portable. In other words, if you leave the group, you cannot take it with you.
3. Group disability coverage is a benefit that can be provided on a discriminatory basis. In other words, you do not have to provide it to all employees and can carve out the physicians and executives for coverage.
4. If the group pays for the coverage with tax-deductible dollars, the benefit is *taxable* if paid to the physician in the event of disability. Instead, if the group pays for the benefit, and declares it as income to the physician, the benefit would be received *tax-free* in the event of disability.

Due to concerns about the lack of portability and the changeable nature of the contract, many medical groups elect not to provide a group disability plan to the physicians. Instead, they reimburse the cost of each physician's individually owned policy. This is better for the physician on many fronts:

1. They can take the coverage with them if they leave the group.
2. The insurance company cannot change the contract.
3. Coverage can be increased on an individual basis if income increases.
4. The definitions of disability provided by individual policies are usually much stronger than group policies.

Because the above is true, many physicians wonder why a group would ever provide a group disability policy. There are two reasons:

1. Group disability coverage in a large group setting does not usually require any underwriting. In other words, you can still get coverage even if your health is sub-par.
2. Group disability coverage can sometimes offer cost savings if the group is large enough to benefit from economies of scale.

For smaller groups, those with less than 20 physicians, it rarely makes sense to institute a group disability plan. Instead, we usually suggest that the group should reimburse a specific dollar amount for disability or long-term care insurance coverage each year. Each physician can then make his or her own decision about the type of coverage to acquire.

For larger groups considering instituting a group disability plan or increasing an existing benefit, a specific process needs to be followed in order to accomplish this correctly.

First, each physician should make sure he or she has acquired as much individually owned disability insurance as desired. Any new group coverage acquired will decrease the amount of individual coverage the physician is eligible to receive. Only at that time should the group coverage amount be increased.

Older physicians within the group may be less interested in disability insurance and more interested in long-term care insurance.

Group Long-Term Care Insurance

Just like disability insurance, long-term care insurance is a benefit that can be provided within a group on a discriminatory basis. Disability insurance is usually recognized as more important for younger physicians who have not yet had the time to build up their own substantial assets. Physicians closer to entering their retirement years often drop disability insurance when it is no longer essential for protecting their families. In these instances, long-term care insurance presents a viable opportunity, and it becomes more attractive tax-wise from a group practice setting.

To understand the opportunity, one must first understand how long-term care insurance is taxed. For individuals, an age table determines what percentage of long-term care insurance premiums can be paid with pre-tax dollars each year.

2012 Federal Long-Term Care Insurance Tax Deductible Limits

Taxpayer's Age at End of Tax Year	2012	2011
40 or Less	$350	$340
More than 40 but not more than 50	$660	$640
More than 50 but not more than 60	$1,310	$1,270
More than 60 but not more than 70	$3,500	$3,390
More than 70	$4,370	$4,240

If purchasing coverage as an individual, the tax deduction available for premiums paid is capped at the amounts shown above, and becomes part of the medical expense deduction. Because medical expenses must exceed 7.5% of one's AGI prior to any tax savings, most physicians are precluded from actually realizing any tax savings.

The options get remarkably better when pursued as a group practice. The extent of the additional tax savings depends on the type of corporation utilized. Partnerships and S-Corporations provide the physician with the opportunity to deduct premiums up to the above dollar limits without regard to the 7.5% AGI threshold. C-Corporations have even more tax incentives available. The C-Corporation can deduct 100% of the premiums paid for long-term care insurance premiums. To maximize this feature, C-Corporations could use a portion of their retained earnings to acquire coverage for the physicians in the practice. By acquiring a 10-pay, or shorter policy, the group can maximize deductions, and pay up a policy that will last for the remainder of the physicians' lives.[93]

Group Life Insurance

Group life insurance can be provided to employees on a pre-tax basis to the practice. Provided the coverage is $50,000 or less of term insurance, the employee has no tax cost. For anything above $50,000 in term insurance, even if the coverage is paid for by the practice, the cost of insurance above this amount must be passed on as a taxable benefit to employees. For this reason, and because group coverage is often more expensive than individual coverage, most groups limit their coverage amount of group life insurance to $50,000. This amount can often be acquired as an add-on benefit to the health insurance plan, with minimal additional cost on the practice's part. Those employees who are healthy are usually better off purchasing coverage on their own.

Voluntary Benefits

Voluntary benefits are those benefits that are not provided to employees directly by the employee but instead are made available at the employee's option and expense. The options for voluntary benefits seem to increase monthly. The goal of any of these benefits is to provide an additional value (time or money saved) to those employees who have the desire to participate in these services.

Again, rather than spending time trying to describe all of the possibilities for voluntary benefits, we want to address the most important voluntary benefits for physicians: dependent care reimbursement arrangements, portable disability insurance for residents, and guaranteed group term life insurance.

Dependent Care Reimbursement Arrangements

Many physicians pay for childcare expenses for their young children so that they can go to work each day. Provided that this childcare makes it possible for both spouses (if married) to work each day, then most Americans have the opportunity to deduct the cost of childcare off of their income for tax purposes. Unfortunately, due to your income being greater than allowable limits, most physicians lose out on a portion of their deduction for these expenses.

However, when a voluntary dependent care reimbursement arrangement is utilized, the physician is no longer subject to the same income restrictions to maintain eligibility for the maximum tax deduction allowable. In other words, by participating in this plan, you could become eligible for tax savings that you were previously losing due to your income being too high. [59]

Portable Disability Insurance for Residents

We have previously covered the importance of disability insurance in several other sections of this book (see pages 36, 43-47). The harsh reality is that many resident physicians coming out of training have medical or family health history that precludes them from qualifying for the important Tier 3 disability coverage we have been discussing. In this instance, residency programs have the opportunity to put in place a win-win solution that benefits the residents and the institution.

The residency program does this by putting in place a portable long-term disability program for its residents. A program such as this has no cost to the residency program, but once in place, most final-year residents qualify to purchase Tier 3 disability insurance protection with no regard for health history.

Recent Example

At one university, more than 50% of the graduates we encountered admitted to having taken anti-anxiety medication, having a needle stick incident, or a miscarriage during pregnancy. The problem was that any of these basic issues precluded them from acquiring strong Tier 3 disability insurance.

The solution was for the residency program to adopt a portable long-term disability insurance plan and make it available to all graduating residents. By doing so, the residents all had access to strong, Tier 3 coverage, without being penalized for taking anti-anxiety medication. There was no cost to the residency program to put this plan in place. All that was required was for them to make sure the graduating residents knew the plan existed. Once the residents reached a point of being within 6 months of graduation, they could elect to purchase coverage at their own expense that stayed with them regardless of where they went for practice.

If done properly, implementing a voluntary long-term disability plan can also save the resident physicians substantial dollars throughout their careers. At the time of the writing of this book, discounts of up to 60% are offered to graduating residents. This discount stays with the physician for as long as he or she owns the policy.

Guaranteed Group Term Life Insurance

Many groups provide a minimal amount of term life insurance to employees free of charge as part of their health insurance benefit. It is important that groups offer additional voluntary life insurance to employees on top of this basic amount. This is because many employees and physicians cannot purchase life insurance on their own merits due to health complications. Instead, a guaranteed plan through the group ignores these health complications and provides access to additional coverage at the physician's own expense.

Executive Benefits and Golden Handcuffs

Replacing key employees is one of the most expensive non-revolving costs a practice or hospital can experience. As a result, many practices could benefit by using executive retention strategies–often referred to as golden handcuffs–to keep their strongest employees with the practice on a long-term basis. Although several golden handcuff strategies exist, they are rarely communicated to employees in an effective manner.

Our favorite approach to date is a concept known as the "Five- or Ten-Year Paid Vacation." Through this approach, the employee is given rights to a five- or ten-year fully paid vacation. The catch is that the vacation is not payable unless they stay with the practice until a predetermined age or length of service. Imagine having ten years' worth of vacation pay saved up on your behalf in exchange for a job well done.[72]

Though it sounds too good to be true, the mechanics have been used for more than a century. This is nothing more than a ten-year pension plan with a much better marketing twist to make it sound a lot more fun. When people think of pensions, they do not get warm and fuzzy feelings, but when they think of vacations, they get much more attached. The great news is this: if you start this plan with ten to twenty years of room to fund it, it can be incredibly cost-effective to offer this benefit. We picture your key employee's next job interview with a prospective employer going something like this: "I'm interested in the possibilities you mentioned, Dr. Roberts, but before we get too far into this conversation, my current group is offering to pay for a ten-year vacation for my family, provided I stay with them for seven more years. Is this something your practice will be able to match?"

---

[72] Thanks to Rick Phillips, President of Phillips Financial Services for his innovative use of this concept.

We cannot imagine that conversation going much further. A great feature of the five- or ten-year paid vacation strategy is that it is completely discriminatory, so you can pick and choose exactly which employees to tap on the shoulder.

The vacation strategy outlined above is just one option of many to provide golden handcuffs or discriminatory benefits to your key people. This is a complex area of planning where few advisors have solid training on the best course of action given the dynamics of your situation.

PRACTICAL APPLICATION

Retirement plans, core, voluntary, and executive benefits present substantial opportunities for most medical practices—whether hospital systems, solo practices, multi-specialty clinics, or mid-size groups—to acquire value that is currently being lost. Unfortunately, this is an area where most employee benefits consultants believe they are competent when the reality is that they are not. Our experience is that few employee benefit firms around the country understand the complexities associated with core, voluntary, and executive benefits, and the physician centric issues and psychology involved with the competing agendas that medical groups face.

When it comes to retirement plans, it is especially important to have competent advisors because the decision makers in your group are held personally liable to see that the fiduciary duties of the plan have been fulfilled to its participants. Our experience is that very few medical groups properly fulfill their fiduciary duties as it relates to their plan design and investment selection. Furthermore, physicians would do well to spend more time addressing these issues and less time trying to defer additional income into a future, unknown tax rate.

Through our constant interaction with physicians, we have developed a short list of professionals around the country that are well qualified to address these concerns for your practice. Our best advice is to connect with us so that we can help to pair you with the best benefits consultant available to solve your unique challenges.

Connect with us by visiting
www.LarsonFinancial.com/Benefits

Wrap Up
Choose Your Team Wisely to Make Success a Reality

---

*"No real action item exists unless you also have
a responsible party, and a deadline."*

Many physicians served as test subjects to read through this book prior to sending it out for publication. They had two consistent responses:
1. They wished they had been confronted with these issues as part of their medical training.
2. They wanted to know what to do next.

This book was written to be educational and practical, but there is no way a book can solve your unique financial challenges. Wealth planning is an ever-changing, complex field that can significantly impact portions of your lifestyle well beyond the financial realms.

As a starting point, spend some time in the *Practical Application* sections at the end of each chapter. These were designed as a springboard to make your conversations with a financial advisor as productive as possible. The next step is to hire a competent advisor to help implement the cost-saving measures outlined in these chapters. The advisor you choose could save or cost you millions of dollars over your lifetime, so this is not a decision that should be taken lightly.

The question becomes, "How should I determine which financial advisor to hire?" Obviously, our hope is that you will consider working with one of our experienced advisors. Working with physicians like you is *all* we do *all* of the time. We understand the unique issues that you face as a doctor because our other clients are also facing them. We believe this level of specialization is crucial for an advisor serving physicians because most of the topics discussed in these pages are specific to your chosen profession, and do not apply to the rest of the population.

We offer the following questions as those that need to be asked before you consider hiring any advisor to serve as the quarterback of your financial life.

Questions to Ask Before Hiring a Financial Advisor:

Q: Do they specialize in working with physicians?

This question is crucial! You want an advisor that works primarily with other clients in similar circumstances to your own. Run away from anyone that gives a vague answer to this question, or claims to be a generalist who can work for anyone. Like an obstetrician trying to complete brain surgery, advisors that work primarily with technology executives would be ill equipped to work with a physician.

The challenge is that many advisors will wrongfully claim to be a specialist with physicians, if a physician is asking the question. To weed out those who are being less than truthful, ask them what they recommend as it relates to your tail coverage. Alternatively, ask them what an RVU is, and see how they respond. Most advisors will not know what you are talking about because they do not spend enough time in your world.

> **This is all we do all the time so our advisors understand the unique financial challenges you face as a physician.**

Q: Are they held to a fiduciary standard?

An advisor can be held to two different standards when it comes to his or her treatment of your situation. Either a standard of *suitability*, or a *fiduciary* standard. A standard of suitability simply requires that the advisor must not blatantly harm you through his or her advice. A fiduciary standard is much more stringent. A fiduciary standard legally requires an advisor to do what is in *your* best interest.

What if you learned a physician was writing a script for cholesterol medication for every patient–whether they had a cholesterol problem or not? Let's pretend no patient would be hurt by this. Would you be appalled to learn that this physician was only suggesting this medication because he would receive a free Caribbean cruise for every 300 scripts written?

The above example is eerily similar to how many advisors operate, selling the same financial products to everyone that walks in their door. This advice might not hurt you–but is it the best thing for your family? Our recommendation is to work with an advisor held to the higher *fiduciary* standard.

Q: What professional credentials do they hold?

These days, anyone loosely related to the financial industry can call him/herself a "financial planner." It is shocking to most physicians that in the financial industry, board certification is *optional.* Most advisors elect not to pursue this important educational track.

Be sure that the firm you decide to hire has on its team advisors that are either Certified Financial Planners (CFP®), Certified Private Wealth Advisors (CPWA®), or Chartered Financial Analysts (CFA). This shows the firm's commitment to high educational standards. It also indicates that the advisors are trained at examining the interconnectedness of your financial and personal lives. Working with a CFP® also means that your advisor is required to disclose their sources of compensation, and any conflicts of interest they may have, as it relates to working with your family.

Having Chartered Financial Analysts (CFA) on the team provides evidence that the firm has professionals with specialty training in the area of investment analysis. It requires a three-year certification process, and hundreds of hours of study to obtain one's CFA. Advisors who pass it command respect within our industry.

Additionally, you may want to ask about any other specialized training the firm has available for its advisors. For example, all of our advisors are required to complete a fellowship prior to working with clients on their own. This way we can monitor their progress, and seek to ensure we have topnotch people representing our good name to the medical community. We also offer specialized training programs to cover advanced issues like asset protection, contract review, and practice management, specifically related to physicians.

When working with a Larson Financial Group advisor, you can be confident that you are working with an advisor that is among the best trained in the industry. Make sure that whomever you work with can make this claim because part of your financial future depends on it.

Q: Are they independent?

Financial advisors are of three types: investment-based advisors, insurance-based advisors, and planning-based advisors. Whether or not the advisor works primarily for you or primarily for a company ultimately determines the differences. Our experience is that most doctors and dentists want an advisor that works directly for them, and not for an investment firm, bank, or insurance company that is demanding product sales quotas.

It is unfortunately very difficult to distinguish among these types of advisors. Imagine a family practice physician holding out her shingle as an anesthesiologist. That would be absurd, but it is exactly what happens in the financial world. The best way we know of to truly determine which type of advisor you are talking with, is to find out who their parent company is. If the parent company is an insurance company, this should be a warning sign that your advisor's primary focus is likely to be on insurance, and their "financial planning" process will be designed to offer you more insurance. If the parent company is an investment firm, do not be surprised when they discuss how well they can beat the market for you, and they do not understand much about the other areas of planning. If the parent company is a bank, likely they will suggest their bank's mutual funds or loan products are the best solution available, even if few other professionals in the industry would speak highly about their products.

A much better decision is to hire an advisor that does not answer directly to a product-pushing parent company, and instead works primarily for you and your family. This is exactly how our advisors operate at Larson Financial Group.

Q: How do they get compensated?

We suggest that you should avoid advisors that are not compensated through fees for their advice. If they do not charge a fee, then the only way they can get compensated is to sell you a product. Even if they do a good job, you'll be stuck wondering if they acted in your best interest.

Fees allow advisors to maintain a level of objectivity that clients desire.

Many of our advisors started out with product-based firms but left them to join us because they liked the idea of not always having to sell a product in order to be fairly compensated for their time.

At Larson Financial Group, our process begins by charging our clients a *reasonable* fee for our time. These fees are what allow us to remain objective and unbiased as it relates to our recommendations for your family. Our clients have confidence in our process, knowing that they have paid us to find the best possible solutions for their family. The commissions that we receive are secondary in nature. They often come through products that we have negotiated discounts for of up to 60% for physicians. Our collective economies of scale working with thousands of specialists around the country give us leverage with many companies that other firms have been unable to duplicate. Our agreement with doctors and dentists also provides a provision that if they are unhappy for any reason whatsoever, then we will refund their planning fee on a year-by-year basis.

Q: Are they willing to disclose conflicts of interest?

This should be the advisor's standard protocol. CFP® practitioners are required to follow this standard. The problem, though, is that this is a rarity in the financial service industry, because the law does not always require it. Would you be disturbed to learn that your advisor's own employee benefits were provided only if he sold enough of one company's products, even if they were not competitive or well-designed? What if you learned your advisor was being given a sizeable quarterly bonus in order to sell one company's investment options over another?

Conflicts of interest like these are prevalent in the financial service industry, and you will never know about them unless your advisor is willing to make a full disclosure.

> **Better yet, find an independent advisor who will give you more objective advice because she has no incentive to offer one product over another.**

Q: Do they have access to institutional products?

Most financial advisors provide the same products that you can acquire for yourself in the normal retail marketplace. Instead, at Larson Financial Group we have negotiated for better pricing on behalf of the thousands of physicians we represent. Our clients have access to a variety of special products not normally available in the general marketplace. The negotiations we do on behalf of our collective physicians are a big part of the value proposition that we offer and can many times offset any direct expenses charged to our clients.

Q: Do they utilize a well-known, third party custodian?

The "custodian" is the company or firm that will actually hold your money or stock certificates. Authors Daniel Goldie, CFA, CFP, and Gordon Murray, suggest:

> "under no circumstances should you work with any advisor that takes custody of your money himself. This is how Bernie Madoff and others were able to steal from their clients." [50]

We concur with this statement. The market has many reputable custodians. The key is to keep the custodian independent from the advisor, since this adds checks and balances into your financial picture, and provides you with an audited monthly statement from someone other than your advisor.

> **By asking these questions, you should be better able to discern discern the true colors of any advisor relationship you are contemplating.**

Again, we hope this book has been informative and helpful. We would be honored to have the opportunity to work with you and your family. We have clients in almost every state, and in many countries around the world. The common thread is that our clients are medical professionals who want to make their finances a balanced area of their life so that they can spend their time on more important things.

An initial consultation with any of our advisors is always free of cost or obligation. This time is an opportunity for all of us to gauge whether your needs and our services are a good match.

To connect with an advisor in your area please visit the following link:

www.LarsonFinancial.com/Advisor

About the Authors

Tom Martin

As a specialist for physicians, Tom has been privileged to provide training for doctors and dentists in some of the top academic programs and private practices around the country. It was through these efforts, and the prompting of numerous clients, that Tom first dreamt of putting this material into an easy-to-explore format for physicians and their spouses.

As a frequent speaker and author, Tom's investment and financial planning advice has been published in medical resources such as *Medical Economics, Physician's Money Digest*, and *Surgical Rounds*. Tom has also spoken to several professional groups on advanced planning topics for physicians, and has completed specialized training in asset-protection planning.

For his graduate work at the Institute of Personal Financial Planning at Kansas State University, Tom was inducted to the Phi Kappa Phi and Kappa Omicron Nu scholastic honor societies. He has also conducted graduate training through the University of Chicago's Booth School of Business and Bethel Theological Seminary. As a professor, he served as the Chairman of Taylor University's CFP® Certification Education Program and Advisory Board after helping the university build and launch Indiana's first CFP® education curriculum for professionals.

Tom is passionate about helping physicians to become more educated decision makers. That's what this book is all about.

Paul Larson

Paul Larson is an innovator for doctors. After working with a medical specialist in his late 40s who was way behind financially, Paul realized that physicians and dentists had unique challenges that were not being properly addressed due to a lack of training for financial professionals.

Paul took action and today, his firm, Larson Financial Group, LLC, is the nation's largest wealth management firm dedicated to exclusively serving the needs of medical professionals. Larson Financial Group is also honored to have more advisors included among *Medical Economics* "Top Advisers for Doctors" than any other firm in the nation.

While continuing to grow a specialized firm that will meet the complex needs of doctors, Paul now sets his sights on building a charitable foundation that will meet the physical, medical, and spiritual needs of orphans around the globe.

Jeffrey Larson

Jeff is a frequent lecturer for many of the nation's top medical training programs. He is sought out often as a negotiator for physician contracts and has been instrumental in developing compensation strategies for the medical industry that meet the objectives of both the physician and the practice.

In addition to his medical contract knowledge, Jeff is widely sought out to provide education for physicians and dentists regarding asset protection, tax planning, investment fundamentals, and estate planning.

Jeff is a primary instructor in Larson Financial Group's fellowship program where financial advisors are taught the specific nuances essential to guiding a physician's financial life. His desire is to impart his knowledge to a future generation of advisors that is well-equipped to address the specific challenges physicians face daily in their financial lives.

Works Cited

1. **Garner, Bryan A. and Black, Henry C.** *Black's Law Dictionary.* St. Paul, MN : West, 2009 Edition.

2. **Scott, Steven K.** *The Richest Man Who Ever Lived: King Solomon's Secrets to Success, Wealth, and Happiness.* Colorado Springs, CO : Waterbrook Press, 2006.

3. Ecclesiastes 2:4-11, 5:10-15; Proverbs 22:7, Proverbs 23:4-5; Haggai 1:6. *NLT Study Bible.* Carol Stream, IL : Tyndale House, 2008.

4. **Sotile, Wayne M. and Sotile, Mary O.** *The Medical Marriage: Sustaining Healthy Relationships for Physicians and Their Families.* Chicago, IL : American Medical Association, 2000.

5. *Unskilled and Unaware of It: How Difficulties in Recognizing One's Own Incompetence Lead to Inflated Self-Assessments.* **Dunning, David and Justin, Kruger.** Washington, D.C. : American Psychological Association, 1999 , Vol. 77.

6. **Montier, James.** *The Folly of Forecasting: Ignore All Economists, Strategists, and Analysts.* London, England : DrKW Macro Research, 2005.

7. **Fincher, David.** *Fight Club.* Fox 2000 Pictures, 1999.

8. **Palms, Peggy.** *The Bankruptcy Solution: How to Eliminate Debt and Rebuild Your Life.* Avon, MA : Adams Media, 2003.

9. **Altfest, Lewis J.** *Personal Financial Planning.* Boston, MA : MacGraw-Hill Irwin, 2007.

10. **Alcorn, Randy C.** *The Treasure Principle.* Colorado Springs, CO : Multnomah, 2008.

11. **Post, Ph.D., Stephen and Neimark, Jill.** *Why Good Things Happen to Good People.* New York, NY : Broadway Books, 2007.

12. **Vickery, M.D., Ryan and Vickery, Rebecca.** *Personal Interview with Dr. Ryan and Mrs. Rebecca Vickery.* 2010 30-September.

13. **Carson, M.D., Ben and Lewis, Gregg.** *The Big Picture: Getting Perspective on What's Really Important in Life.* Grand Rapids, MI : Zondervan, 1999.

14. **Foley, Eric.** *Coach Your Champions: The Transformational Giving Approach to Major Donor Fundraising.* Colorado Springs, CO : .W Publishing, 2009.

15. **Logan, J.T.** The Mayo Clinic. *The Free Methodist.* 1931 13-February.

16. *Safe Savings Rates: A New Approach to Retirement Planning over the Life Cycle.* **Pfau, Wade D.** Washington, DC : Financial Planning Association, May 2011, Journal of Financial Planning.

17. **AAMC.** *2010 Debt Fact Card.* Washington, D.C. : Association of American Medical Colleges, 2010.

18. **Bureau, U.S. Census.** *U.S. Census Web Site.* [Online] [Cited: 2011 8-June.] http://www.census.gov.

19. **Kirwan, J.D., LL.M. Adam O.** *The Asset Protection Guide for Florida Physicians: The Ultimate Guide to Protecting Your Wealth in Difficult Economic Times.* Orlando, FL : The Kirwan Law Firm, Updated and Revised for 2010.

20. **Adkisson, Jay D. and Riser, Christopher M.** Creditor-Debtor State Exemption Chart. *Asset Protection Book.* [Online] [Cited: 2011 8-June.] http://www.creditorexemption.com.

21. **Riser, Christopher M. and Adkisson, Jay D.** *Asset Protection: Concepts and Strategies for Protecting Your Wealth.* New York, NY : McGraw-Hill, 2004.

22. *Publication 936: Home Mortgage Interest Deduction.* Department of the Treasury, Internal Revenue Service. Washington, D.C. : Internal Revenue Service, 2010.

23. **Martin, CFP®, Thomas S.** *Life's Toughest Battles.* St. Louis, MO : Larson Financial Group, LLC, 2008.

24. National Clearinghouse for Long-Term Care Information. *U.S. Department of Health and Human Services.* [Online] 2011 8-April. [Cited: 2011 8-June.] http://www.longtermcare.gov/LTC/Main_Site/Paying_LTC/Private_Programs/LTC_Insurance/index.aspx#SPLTCIP.

25. **Holm, Jeanne M.** Quotes Related to Knowledge Management or Collaboration. *NASA.gov.* [Online] 2010 30-September. [Cited: 2011 20-June.] http://km.nasa.gov/whatis/KM_Quotes.html.

26. **Murray, Nick.** *Simple Wealth, Inevitable Wealth.* Mattituck, NY : Nick Murray Press, 2008.

27. **DALBAR.** *Quantitative Analysis of Investor Behavior (QAIB).* Boston, MA : DALBAR, 2001, 2006, and 2011 Updates.

28. *Publication 590: Individual Retirement Arrangements.* Department of the Treasury, Internal Revenue Service. Washington, D.C. : Internal Revenue Service, 2010.

29. *Do Required Minimum Distributions Endanger 'Safe' Portfolio Withdrawal Rates?* **Spitzer, Ph.D., John J.** 8, Denver, CO : Journal of Financial Planning, 2008 , Vol. 21.

30. **Bruno, CFP, Maria A. and Jaconetti, CPA, CFP, Colleen.** *The Rules for Roth Conversions are Changing in 2010.* Valley Forge, PA : The Vanguard Group, Inc., 2009.

31. **Jenab, J.D. Lawrence.** *IRS Provides Guidance on In-Plan Roth Conversions.* Overland Park, KS : Spencer Fane Publications, 2011.

32. **Milevsky, Moshe A.** *The Calculus of Retirement Income.* New York, NY : Cambridge University Press, 2006.

33. **Milevsky, Mosha A.** Confessions of a VA Critic. *Research Magazine.* 2007 1-January.

34. **State of Michigan.** *2012 Pension Withholding Guide.* Department of Treasury. Lansing : s.n., 2011. 4927 (11-11).

35. **Swedroe, Larry E. and Kizer, Jared.** *The Only Guide to Alternative Investments You'll Ever Need.* New York, NY : Bloomberg Press, 2008.

36. **Swedroe, Larry E.** *The Quest for Alpha.* Hoboken, NJ : John Wiley & Sons, Inc., 2011.

37. **Swensen, David.** *Unconventional Success.* New York, NY : Free Press, 2005.

38. **Center for Research in Security Prices.** *Survivor-Bias-Free US Mutual Fund Guide.* Chicago, IL : Chicago Booth, 2011.

39. *Luck versus Skill in the Cross-Section of Mutual Fund Returns.* **Fama, Eugene F. and French, Kenneth R.** 5, Aldan, PA : the American Finance Association, 2010 , Journal of Finance, Vol. 65.

40. **Morningstar®.** *The Morningstar Rating™ for Funds.* Chicago, IL : Morningstar, Inc., 2008.

41. **Wellington, Weston.** *Deconstructing Berkshire Hathaway.* Austin, TX : Dimensional Fund Advisors LP, 2011.

42. **Ramirez, Anthony.** Surprise at Magellan Fund: Lynch Successor is Leaving. *The New York Times.* 1992 30-April.

43. **Buffett, Warren.** *Chairman's Letter in the Annual Report to Investors.* Omaha, NE : Berkshire Hathaway, 2006.

44. *Determinants of Portfolio Performance II: An Update.* **Brinson, Gary P., Singer, Brian D. and Beebower, Gilbert L.** Charlottesville, VA : CFA Institute, 1991 May/June, Financial Analysts Journal.

45. **Dimensional Fund Advisors.** *Matrix Book.* Austin, TX : Dimensional Fund Advisors, 2011.

46. **Shell, Adam.** Will Stocks' "Lost Decade" Usher in Another Bull Market? *USA Today.* January 4, 2010.

47. **Weidner, David.** The Lost Decade of Stock Investing. *The Wall Street Journal.* October 15, 2009.

48. *Publication 17: Your Federal Income Tax.* Department of the Treasury, Internal Revenue Service. Washington, D.C. : Internal Revenue Service, 2010.

49. **Zweig, Jason.** *Your Money and Your Brain: How the New Science of Neuroeconomics Can Help Make You Rich.* New York, NY : Simon & Schuster, 2007.

50. **Goldie, CFA, CFP, Daniel C. and Murray, Gordon S.** *The Investment Answer: Learn to Manage Your Money & Protect Your Financial Future.* New York, NY : Business Plus, 2011.

51. **Wikipedia.** William E. Vaughan. *Wikipedia.* [Online] 2011 20-September. [Cited: 2011 05-October.] http://en.wikipedia.org/wiki/William_E._Vaughan.

52. *Publication 970: Tax Benefits for Higher Education.* Department of the Treasury, Internal Revenue Service. Washington, D.C. : Internal Revenue Service, 2010.

53. **Kantrowitz, Mark.** Section 529 Plans. *FinAid!* [Online] 2011. [Cited: 2001 8-June.] www.finaid.org/savings/529plans.

54. **Hand, Billings Learned.** *Helvering v. Gregory.* 69 F .2d 809, 810-11, s.l. : Second Circuit, 1934.

55. America Celebrates Tax Freedom Day. *Tax Foundation.* [Online] 2011. [Cited: 2011 8-June.] http://www.taxfoundation.org/taxfreedomday.

56. *Publication 526: Charitable Contributions.* Department of the Treasury, Internal Revenue Service. Washington, D.C. : Internal Revenue Service, 2010.

57. *Publication 529: Miscellaneous Deductions.* Department of the Treasury, Internal Revenue Service. Washington, D.C. : Internal Revenue Service, 2010.

58. *Publication 502: Medical and Dental Expenses.* Department of the Treasury, Internal Revenue Service. Washington, D.C. : Internal Revenue Service, 2010.

59. *Publication 503: Child and Dependent Care Expenses.* Department of the Treasury, Internal Revenue Service. Washington, D.C. : Internal Revenue Service, 2010.

60. **Saxton, Jim (R-NJ), Chairman.** *The Alternative Minimum Tax for Individuals: A Growing Burden.* Washington, D.C. : Joint Economic Committee, United States Congress, 2001.

61. **Shakin, Joshua.** *The Individual Alternative Minimum Tax.* Congressional Budget Office, Tax Analysis Division. Washington, D.C. : Congressional Budget Office, 2010.

62. **Forefield, Inc.** *Net Unrealized Appreciation: The Untold Story.* Marlboro, MA : Forefield, Inc., 2011.

63. **Meyer, Eric.** *Personal Interview with Eric Meyer of MedTax, Inc.* St. Louis, MO, 2011 3-March.

64. **Elliot, Jim.** *The Journals of Jim Elliot.* Grand Rapids, MI : Revell, 2002.

65. **Cochell, Perry L. and Zeeb, Rodney C.** *Beating the Midas Curse.* West Linn, OR : Heritage Institute Press, LLC, 2005.

66. **Kilbourn, E. Michael.** *Disinherit the IRS.* Franklin Lakes, NJ : The Career Press, Inc., 2003.

67. **Fontaine, Constance J.** *Fundamentals of Estate Planning.* Bryn Mawr, PA : The American College Press, 2006.

68. **Mintz, Esq., Robert J.** *Asset Protection for Physicians and High-Risk Business Owners.* Fallbrook, CA : Francis O'Brien & Sons Publishing Company, Inc., 2007.

69. **Cassingham, Randy.** *The True Stella Awards: Honoring Real Cases of Greedy Opportunists, Frivolous Lawsuits, and the Law Run Amok.* New York, NY : Penguin Group, 2006.

70. *HONDA OF AMERICA MANUFACTURING INC. v. NORMAN.* No. 01-00-01263-CV., www.findlaw.com : Court of Appeals Texas, Houston (1st District), 2003.

71. *McKENZIE v. HAWAII PERMANENTE MEDICAL GROUP INC.* No. 23268., www.findlaw.com : Supreme Court of Hawaii, 2002.

72. **Cassingham, Randy.** The 2005 True Stella Awards Winners. *StellaAwards.com.* [Online] 2006 31-January. [Cited: 2011 22-June.] http://stellaawards.com/2005.html.

73. **Yates, Jon.** Intruder's Death Partially Blamed on Bar Owners. *Chicago Tribune.* 2003 25-February.

74. **Sahadi, Jeanne.** Why O.J. May Pay. *CNN Money.* 2000 7-September.

75. **Gerber, Michael E.** *The E-Myth Physician.* New York, NY : HarperCollins Publishers Inc., 2003.

76. **Balkenbusch, Howard "Skip".** Fort Wayne, IN, 2010 8-December.

77. **Berman, Saul, Davidson, Steven and Blitz, Amy.** *Succeeding in the New Economic Environment.* Somers, NY : IBM Corporation, 2009.

78. **Maxwell, John C.** *Be A People Person: Effective Leadership through Effective Relationships.* Colorado Springs, CO : David C. Cook, 2007.

79. **Covey, Stephen R., Whitman, Robert and England, Breck.** *Predictable Results in Unpredictable Times.* Salt Lake City, UT : Franklin Covey Publishing, 2009.

80. **Berry, Leonard L. and Seltman, Kent D.** *Management Lessons from Mayo Clinic: Inside One of the World's Most Admired Service Organizations.* New York, NY : McGraw-Hill, 2008.

81. **Collins, Jim.** *Good to Great.* New York, NY : Harper Business, 2001.

82. **Kolbe, Kathy.** *Pure Instinct.* s.l. : Monumentus Press, 2004.

83. *Marriage: Getting From Where We are to Where We Want to Be.* **Hawks, Richard W.** Fort Wayne, IN : The Chapel, 2011.

84. **Patterson, Kerry, et al.** *Crucial Conversations.* New York, NY : McGraw-Hill, 2002.

85. **Grimme, Don and Sheryl.** *The New Manager's Tool Kit: 21 Things You Need to Know to Hit the Ground Running.* New York, NY : AMACOM, 2009.

86. **Pritchard, Scott.** All Fiduciaries are Not the Same - Part II. *www. advisorsaccess.com.* [Online] 2010 25-August. [Cited: 2011 15-June.] http://www.advisorsaccess.com/blogs/pritchard.php.

87. **Simon, W. Scott.** Fiduciary Focus: Active vs. Passive Investing (Part 4). *Morningstar Advisor.* [Online] 2005 25-May. [Cited: 2011 15-June.] http://www.morningstaradvisor.com/articles/fcarticle. asp?s=&docId=4086&pgNo=0.

88. **Charles Schwab Corporation.** Advice Matters: New Charles Schwab Study Demonstrates Positive Impact of Professional Advice on 401(k) Investor Behavior. *Press Release.* 2010 15-September.

89. *The Tyranny of Choice - Why 401(k) Plans are Failing and the Cure to Save Them.* **N. Scott Pritchard, AIFA.** 1, New York, NY : Aspen Publishers, 2008, Journal of Pension Benefits, Vol. 16.

90. **Collins, Margaret.** Labor Department Requires 401(k) Fee Disclosure. *Bloomberg.* 2010 14-October.

91. **Winn, CLU, ChFC, Paul J.** *Healthcare Reform: Critical Aspects of the Patient Protection and Affordable Care Act.* Williamsburg, VA : WebCE, 2010.

92. **Ellsasser, Edward C.** *Personal Interview with Edward Ellsasser.* Tampa, Florida, 2011 30-June.

93. **The American Association of Long-Term Care Insurance.** Long-Term Care Insurance Tax-Deductibility Rules. *American Association for Long-Term Care Insurance Consumer's Information Center.* [Online] 2011. [Cited: 2011 8-July.] http://www.aaltci.org/long-term-care-insurance/learning-center/tax-for-business.php.

94. **Leimberg, Stephan R., et al.** *Tools & Techniques of Estate Planning.* Cincinnati, OH : The National Underwriter Company, 2006.

17268755R00128

Made in the USA
Charleston, SC
03 February 2013